Moving Through the Shadows:

A Self-Help Program for Healing Depression, Anxiety, and Anger in 8 Weeks with Somatic Therapy Techniques

Dr. Richard Nongard, Psy.D.

Moving Through the Shadows: A Self-Help Program for Healing Depression, Anxiety, and Anger in 8 Weeks with Somatic Therapy Techniques

Dr. Richard K. Nongard , Psy.D.

Copyright © 2025 Dr. Richard K. Nongard

ISBN: 979-8-9876484-6-9

All Rights Reserved.

No part of this publication may be reproduced, distributed, or transmitted in any form or by any means, including photocopying, recording, or other electronic or mechanical methods, without the prior written permission from the author, except in the case of brief quotations embodied in critical reviews and certain other noncommercial uses permitted by copyright law.

Dr. Richard K. Nongard
Nevada Hypnosis LLC
6130 W. Flamingo Rd. STE 123
Las Vegas, NV 89103

(702) 418-3332

www.ExpertHypnosis.com

Dr. Richard Nongard is available to speak at your business or conference event on a variety of topics. Email Dr. Nongard at richard@nongard.com for booking information.

Written by a Leading Expert with 35+ Years' Experience

Dr. Richard K. Nongard is an ICBCH certified professional hypnotist, a licensed marriage and family therapist, and holds a doctor of psychology degree. He is a university professor with over 35 years of experience in counseling, professional hypnosis, and educating other professionals. He is an expert at helping people create lasting success. He has been a TEDx speaker, he is a popular author with over 35 books to his credit, and his meditation, somatic therapy, and self-hypnosis videos have been seen by more than four million people.

Dr. Richard K. Nongard is the expert whom other professionals study with and learn advanced methods of professional hypnosis and somatic approaches to hypnotherapy. In this book, he reveals the strategies that actually work and how you can do them at home. Everything is explained step-by-step. When you are finished with this book, you will have a new resource that you can tap into for the rest of your life.

Do you want Dr. Richard K. Nongard to be the motivational speaker at your next event?

Email richard@nongard.com or visit ExpertHypnosis.com

Table of Contents

Introduction: Understanding the Hidden Connection 1

Chapter 1: Understanding the Three Faces of Emotional Pain . 9

Chapter 2: Why Emotional Suffering Feels So Impossible to Escape 17

Chapter 3: The 8-Week Protocol for Emotional Transformation 29

Chapter 4: Week 1: Developing Somatic Awareness—The Foundation of Integration 43

Chapter 5: Week 2: Nervous System Regulation—Building Your Internal Resources 63

Chapter 6: Week 3: Emotional Integration—Transforming Your Relationship with Feeling 85

Chapter 7: Week 4: Somatic Cognitive Integration—Bridging Body and Mind 109

Chapter 8: Week 5: Relational Healing—Connection as Medicine 135

Chapter 9: Week 6: Meaning and Purpose Integration—Connecting to Something Larger 165

Chapter 10: Week 7: Integration and Daily Practice—Making Transformation Sustainable 195

Chapter 11: Week 8: Embodied Resilience—Thriving Through Life's Challenges 225

Chapter 12: Real Stories of Transformation 263

Chapter 13: Your Journey Begins Now—Stepping Into Embodied Emotional Intelligence 277

Introduction

Understanding the Hidden Connection

Have you ever noticed how your chest tightens when you're anxious, how your shoulders slump when you're depressed, or how your jaw clenches when you're angry? What if I told you that these three emotions—depression, anxiety, and anger—are not separate enemies to battle but different expressions of the same underlying disconnection between your mind and body?

Welcome to *Moving Through the Shadows*. This isn't just another self-help book with temporary fixes. This is a comprehensive 8-week protocol for emotional transformation that addresses a fundamental truth: **Mind and body are inseparable**, and lasting healing happens when we honor this connection.

For too long, we've been taught to treat our emotions as purely mental experiences, to "think our way out" of feeling bad. But what if the key to emotional freedom lies not in conquering your thoughts but in reuniting with your body's innate wisdom? What if depression, anxiety, and anger are simply your body's different ways of telling you the same thing—that something needs attention, care, and healing?

The Revolutionary Understanding: Three Faces of One Experience

Consider this: Depression often manifests as a collapse inward—slumped posture, shallow breathing, and a sense of heaviness. Anxiety typically shows up as restless energy—racing heart, tense muscles, scattered thoughts. Anger frequently appears as explosive tension—clenched fists, rigid stance, burning sensations.

While these may seem like completely different experiences, they share something profound. They're all responses to disconnection—disconnection from our bodies, from our authentic needs, and from our sense of safety and belonging in the world. They're different languages your nervous system uses to communicate the same underlying message: "Something here needs healing."

This understanding changes everything. Instead of fighting three separate battles, you can learn one integrated approach that addresses the root cause of emotional suffering.

Alma's Transformation Story

Let me tell you about Alma. At 50, she had spent decades cycling between what she called her "three demons"—the crushing weight of depression after losing her mother and husband, the constant anxiety about her future, and the sudden bursts of anger that seemed to come from nowhere and frightened her.

"I felt like I was living in three different bodies," Alma told me. "The depressed body that could barely move, the anxious body that couldn't sit still, and the angry body that felt dangerous. I never understood they were all trying to tell me the same thing."

Throughout this 8-week protocol, Alma learned to listen to her body's messages instead of fighting them. She discovered that her depression was her nervous system's way of protecting her from overwhelming grief, her anxiety was alerting her to unmet needs for security, and her anger was actually a healthy response to years of suppressing her authentic self.

Eight weeks later, Alma described a profound shift: "I'm not saying I never feel sad, worried, or upset anymore. But now these feelings move through me instead of getting stuck in me. I've learned to work with my body instead of against it, and it's changed everything."

My Own Journey: From Fragmentation to Integration

I should be honest with you from the start. I'm not just a therapist who studied emotions in textbooks. I've lived with the cycle of depression, anxiety, and anger for most of my life. There were times when I felt trapped in my own body—exhausted by depression, jittery with anxiety, then surprised by sudden rage that seemed to come from nowhere.

I tried everything: talk therapy, medication, meditation, exercise, and nutrition changes. Each approach helped a little, but nothing created lasting transformation until I discovered what I now call "somatic-emotional integration"—the practice of healing emotions through the body.

I began to understand that my depression wasn't a mental illness to be cured, my anxiety wasn't a disorder to be eliminated, and my anger wasn't a character flaw to be suppressed. They were all my body's attempts to communicate important information about my life, my relationships, and my needs.

Over years of both personal healing and professional practice, I developed this 8-week protocol that has now helped hundreds of people transform their relationship with difficult emotions. The secret isn't in conquering these feelings—it's in learning to dance with them.

About This Transformation Protocol

Moving Through the Shadows is your personal guide to emotional transformation through somatic awareness and integration. Originally developed as a clinical treatment framework, this 8-week protocol has been refined into a comprehensive self-help system that anyone can follow at home, while remaining an invaluable resource for therapists and coaches working with clients.

This approach goes far beyond traditional cognitive methods by centering the body's wisdom on emotional healing. You'll learn that lasting change happens not through thinking differently, but through **feeling differently in your body**. By developing a new relationship with physical sensations, nervous system responses, and embodied awareness, you'll discover that emotional transformation is not only possible—it's your birthright.

What You'll Discover Inside

A Complete 8-Week Transformation System: Clear, week-by-week guidance that takes you from emotional overwhelm to embodied resilience, with each week building naturally on the previous one.

Somatic Integration Practices: Revolutionary exercises that teach you to work with your body's natural healing capacity, including breathwork, gentle movement, nervous system regulation, and trauma-informed body awareness.

The Three-Emotion Connection Map: Tools to understand how depression, anxiety, and anger are connected in your unique system and how healing one transforms them all.

Daily Embodiment Practices: Simple, powerful exercises you can do anywhere to stay connected to your body's wisdom and maintain emotional balance.

Real-World Integration Strategies: Practical applications for maintaining your transformation in relationships, work, and daily life challenges.

Crisis Navigation Tools: Body-based techniques for moving through intense emotional episodes with grace and self-compassion.

How to Use This Protocol

This book is designed as a complete self-transformation system. Each week includes specific practices, reflection exercises, and integration assignments that work together to create lasting change. You can absolutely use this protocol on your own—many people have experienced profound transformation working independently with these materials.

However, this system is also powerful when used with professional support. If you're a therapist, coach, or healing practitioner, you can use this protocol as a treatment framework while adapting it to your clients' unique needs. I especially encourage practitioners to engage with these practices personally—the most effective guides are those who embody the transformation they're facilitating.

What Makes This Approach Revolutionary?

There are countless books about managing depression, controlling anxiety, and handling anger. So why this one? Because most approaches treat these emotions as separate problems to be solved, rather than recognizing them as interconnected expressions of the same underlying disconnection.

This protocol integrates four essential dimensions of healing:

1. **Somatic Awareness:** Learning to listen to your body's wisdom and work with your nervous system's natural capacity for regulation and resilience.

2. **Emotional Integration:** Understanding that all emotions—including difficult ones—carry important information and can be allies in your healing journey.

3. **Relational Healing:** Recognizing that emotional well-being is deeply connected to how we relate to ourselves and others and developing skills for authentic connection.

4. **Meaning-Making:** Discovering that emotional transformation often involves connecting with something larger than yourself—whether you call it purpose, spirituality, or simply love.

When these four dimensions work together, they create what I call "embodied transformation"—change that happens not just in your thoughts but in your cells, your breath, your posture, and your entire way of being in the world.

Important Safety Information

While this protocol offers powerful tools for transformation, please remember that severe depression, anxiety, or anger issues may require professional support. If you're having thoughts of harming yourself or others, please reach out to a crisis helpline or mental health professional immediately. This protocol works beautifully alongside appropriate medical and therapeutic care—it's not meant to replace professional treatment when needed.

Your Journey of Transformation Begins Now

Over the next eight weeks, we'll work together to revolutionize your relationship with difficult emotions. You'll learn to see your body as an ally rather than an enemy, to understand your emotions as messengers rather than problems, and to experience the profound peace that comes from mind-body integration.

Each week includes:

- Clear explanations of what's happening in your nervous system.
- Gentle somatic practices to build body awareness.
- Integration exercises for daily life.
- Reflection prompts to deepen your understanding.
- Resources for continued growth.

This isn't always easy work. There will be days when you want to go back to old patterns, when the practices feel uncomfortable, when you question whether change is really possible. This is all normal and part of the process. What matters is that you keep returning to the practices, trusting in your body's innate capacity for healing.

Remember Alma? Her transformation didn't happen overnight. She had days of doubt, moments of resistance, and times when she wanted to give up. But she kept coming back to the practices, and gradually, her entire relationship with emotion shifted from fear to curiosity and from resistance to flow.

You have this same capacity for transformation. Whether you've struggled with depression, anxiety, anger, or all three—whether this is a new challenge or a lifelong pattern—this protocol offers a path to embodied emotional freedom.

Your body is not broken. Your emotions are not enemies. Your healing is not only possible—it's waiting for you to begin.

Transform your relationship with emotion. Reclaim your body's wisdom. Let's begin this journey together, moving through the shadows toward the integration and peace that await on the other side.

Chapter 1

Understanding the Three Faces of Emotional Pain

I couldn't get out of bed. Not because I was physically ill but because the crushing weight of depression had settled into my chest like concrete. My heart was racing with anxiety about everything I wasn't doing, and underneath it all, anger simmered—at myself, at my situation, at feeling so powerless. The room was bright with morning sunlight, but inside my body, I felt trapped in a storm of conflicting sensations and emotions.

What I didn't understand then was that these three emotional states—depression, anxiety, and anger—weren't separate problems attacking me from different directions. They were all expressions of the same fundamental disconnection: the split between my mind and body that had been widening for years.

As I lay there that morning, I began to notice something remarkable. When the depressive heaviness peaked, my breathing became shallow and my shoulders collapsed inward.

When anxiety spiked, my chest tightened and my thoughts raced. When anger flashed through me, my jaw clenched and my hands formed fists. My body was speaking a language I had never learned to understand.

This realization became the foundation of everything I'm about to share with you—a revolutionary understanding that has transformed not only my own life but the lives of hundreds of people who have followed this 8-week protocol for emotional transformation.

The Hidden Unity Behind Emotional Suffering

What if I told you that depression, anxiety, and anger are not three separate enemies to battle but three different expressions of the same underlying condition? What if the key to healing all three lies not in fighting them but in understanding the language they're speaking through your body?

This understanding changes everything. Instead of feeling overwhelmed by multiple emotional problems, you can focus on healing the root cause: the disconnection between your conscious mind and your body's innate wisdom.

Consider this: Depression often manifests as a collapse inward—slumped posture, shallow breathing, and a sense of heaviness that seems to pull you down into yourself. Anxiety typically shows up as activation—racing heart, tense muscles, and a restless energy that can't find release. Anger frequently appears as explosive tension—clenched jaw, rigid stance, and heat rising through your body.

While these may seem completely different, they share something profound: **they're all your nervous system's attempts to communicate that something needs attention.**

They're different languages your body uses to tell you the same essential message: "We're not integrated. Mind and body are working against each other instead of together."

Are You Living in Three Different Bodies?

As you read this, I invite you to check in on your own experience. Do you recognize what I call "the three-body experience"?

The Depressed Body: Heavy limbs that feel like lead weights. Shoulders that curl inward as if protecting your heart. Breathing that barely fills the top of your lungs. A sense of being trapped inside yourself, watching life happen from behind glass.

The Anxious Body: Muscles that never fully relax. A heart that races even when you're sitting still. Breath that catches in your throat. Energy that feels like electricity with nowhere to go, leaving you simultaneously exhausted and wired.

The Angry Body: Jaw muscles that ache from clenching. Hands that form fists without a conscious decision. Heat that rises from your belly to your face. A sense of being ready to fight or flee, even when there's no real threat present.

If you're nodding as you read this, you're beginning to understand something crucial: **These aren't just emotional states—they're embodied experiences.** And because they live in your body, they can be transformed through body-based healing practices.

Maya's Three-Body Transformation

Let me tell you about Maya, a 38-year-old who came to understand this connection through her own journey with the 8-week protocol. When we first spoke, she described feeling like she was "living in three different bodies that were all fighting each other."

"In the morning, I'd wake up with that familiar depression weight on my chest," she told me. "By noon, anxiety would kick in about all the things I wasn't getting done. By evening, I'd be angry—at myself, at my situation, and at feeling so out of control. I felt like I was being torn apart from the inside."

Maya had tried traditional approaches—therapy focused on changing her thoughts, medications that helped somewhat but left her feeling disconnected, and mindfulness practices that she couldn't sustain when emotions were intense. Each approach helped a little, but nothing addressed the fundamental problem: her mind and body were operating as separate systems instead of as one integrated whole.

When Maya began the 8-week protocol, she started with simple body awareness practices. At first, she was skeptical. "How can paying attention to my breathing help when my brain chemistry is the problem?" she asked.

But as she learned to track the physical sensations of her emotional states, something remarkable began to happen. She discovered that her depression, anxiety, and anger all had early warning signs that showed up in her body before her mind fully registered them:

- The slight tightening in her chest that preceded anxiety.
- The subtle collapse in her posture that signaled approaching depression.
- The tension in her jaw that meant anger was building.

By week four, Maya was learning to work with these physical signals instead of against them. She developed what she called her "body compass"—the ability to sense what her nervous system needed at any given moment and respond with appropriate somatic practices.

"I'm not saying I never feel depressed, anxious, or angry anymore," Maya reported after completing the eight weeks. "But now these feelings move through me instead of getting stuck in me. I've learned that my body isn't the enemy—it's been trying to help me all along. I just never learned its language."

The Revolutionary Understanding: Mind and Body Are One

Here's what most approaches to emotional healing miss: **Mind and body are not separate systems that influence each other—they are one integrated system expressing itself through different channels.**

When you feel depressed, it's not just your brain producing sad thoughts while your body remains neutral. Your entire nervous system is in a state of withdrawal and conservation. Your posture, breathing, muscle tension, and even cellular processes all participate in this state.

When you experience anxiety, it's not just worried thoughts racing through your mind. Your entire system is activated for threat detection and response. Your body is preparing for action even when your conscious mind can't identify what action to take.

When anger arises, it's not just an emotional reaction to circumstances. Your entire physiology is mobilizing energy for protection and boundary-setting, even when there may be no external threat requiring such a response.

This understanding is revolutionary because it means that lasting emotional transformation must involve the body. You cannot think your way out of depression, anxiety, or anger—you must **feel and move** your way through them.

What You'll Discover in This 8-Week Journey

This protocol will guide you through a complete transformation of your relationship with emotional pain. Instead of fighting against depression, anxiety, and anger, you'll learn to work with them as allies in your healing process.

Week 1–2: Foundation Building You'll develop basic somatic awareness skills, learn to recognize how different emotional states live in your body, and begin to establish safety and grounding practices.

Week 3–4: Integration Practices You'll learn specific techniques for working with the physical patterns of depression, anxiety, and anger, discovering how to shift these states through body-based interventions.

Week 5–6: Relational Healing You'll explore how emotional patterns affect your relationships and develop skills for maintaining integration while connecting authentically with others.

Week 7–8: Sustainable Transformation You'll create a personalized practice for maintaining mind-body integration and develop tools for navigating life's inevitable challenges without losing your center.

Throughout this journey, you'll work with several revolutionary concepts:

Pendulation: Learning to move your attention between areas of distress and areas of ease in your body, building resilience and emotional flexibility.

Somatic Resourcing: Developing your body's natural capacity for self-regulation and healing through targeted awareness practices.

Emotional Alchemy: Transforming stuck emotional patterns by working directly with their physical manifestations.

Integration Practices: Combining breathwork, movement, and awareness to create lasting changes in your nervous system's default patterns.

Your Body as Your Greatest Ally

Perhaps the most radical shift you'll experience through this protocol is recognizing your body not as the source of your emotional problems but as your greatest ally in healing them.

Your body has been trying to communicate with you all along. The heaviness of depression is your nervous system's attempt to conserve energy when it perceives overwhelming demand. The activation of anxiety is your system's way of preparing you for challenges it senses approaching. The mobilization of anger is your body's attempt to protect your boundaries and authentic self.

These aren't pathological responses—they're intelligent attempts at survival and self-care. The problem isn't that these responses occur, but that they've become stuck patterns disconnected from present-moment reality.

Through this 8-week protocol, you'll learn to:

- Recognize these patterns as they arise.
- Work with them skillfully instead of against them.
- Transform stuck patterns into flowing, adaptive responses.
- Develop an embodied sense of emotional resilience.

The Journey Begins with One Breath

The path to emotional transformation doesn't require you to become a different person. It requires you to become more fully yourself—integrated, embodied, and responsive to life rather than reactive to old patterns.

This journey begins with something as simple as one conscious breath. As you breathe right now, notice what happens in your body. Does your chest expand? Does your belly soften? Do your shoulders release slightly? This is your first taste of mind-body integration—your conscious awareness directing your body's response in this moment.

Depression, anxiety, and anger have taught you to live in separation—mind against body, thoughts against feelings, and intention against action. This protocol will teach you to live in integration, where all parts of yourself work together in harmony.

The shadows you've been moving through aren't your enemy. They're your teachers, showing you exactly where integration needs to happen. In the next chapter, we'll begin the practical work of building the foundation for this transformation through somatic awareness practices.

Remember: you don't need to be fixed because you're not broken. You need to be integrated because wholeness is your natural state. Let's begin the journey home to yourself.

Chapter 2

Why Emotional Suffering Feels So Impossible to Escape

"I've tried everything," Sarah told me, her voice oscillating between the flat monotone of depression and the tight urgency of anxiety. "Medication for depression, therapy for anger management, and meditation for anxiety. Sometimes, I feel better for a little while, but it's like playing whack-a-mole. I fix one thing, and two others pop up." She paused, her hands clenching into fists—a gesture I'd learned to recognize as her anger trying to break through. "What's wrong with me? Why can't I just be normal like everyone else?"

Sarah had been cycling through what she called her "emotional storm" for twelve years. She'd tried treating her depression with antidepressants, her anxiety with antianxiety medications, and her anger with cognitive behavioral therapy. She'd done anger management courses, mindfulness training for anxiety, and talk therapy for depression. Each approach helped somewhat, but none addressed the fundamental problem: **These weren't three separate issues—they were three faces of the same underlying disconnection.**

"The worst part," she confessed, "is that working on one emotion seems to make the others worse. When I suppress my anger, I get more depressed. When I try to push through depression with activity, my anxiety spikes. I feel like I'm trapped in an emotional prison with no way out."

If Sarah's story sounds familiar, you're not alone. The cycle of hope, partial improvement, relapse, and deeper despair is painfully common among people struggling with the depression-anxiety-anger triad. And there's a crucial reason for this pattern—one that has nothing to do with personal failure and everything to do with how our culture misunderstands the nature of emotional suffering.

The Fragmentation Trap: Treating Symptoms Instead of the Source

Our medical and therapeutic systems have created what I call "the fragmentation trap"—the tendency to treat depression, anxiety, and anger as separate disorders requiring separate solutions. This approach seems logical on the surface, but it misses something fundamental: **These three emotional states are interconnected expressions of the same underlying mind-body disconnection.**

Consider how you and most people navigate this terrain:

- **Monday**: You feel depressed, so you try antidepressants or therapy focused on negative thinking.
- **Wednesday**: Anxiety spikes, so you add antianxiety medication or breathing exercises.

- **Friday**: Anger erupts, so you attempt anger management techniques or suppression strategies.
- **Sunday**: You're exhausted from managing three different "problems" and confused about why nothing seems to work long-term.

This fragmented approach is like trying to treat a fever, headache, and fatigue as three separate illnesses when they're all symptoms of the flu. You end up with a medicine cabinet full of partial solutions while the underlying condition remains unaddressed.

The Quick-Fix Culture That Keeps Us Stuck

We live in a culture that promises immediate relief from emotional discomfort. These messages bombard us constantly, for example:

- **Pharmaceutical ads** show people transforming from anxious to calm, depressed to happy, or angry to peaceful within days of starting medication.
- **Social media influencers** claim their programs will "cure anxiety in twenty-one days" or "eliminate anger forever."
- **Self-help gurus** promote techniques that promise to "think your way out of depression" when the research tells us thinking about anger, depression, and anxiety is just one part of the formula.
- **Wellness trends** suggest that the right supplement, diet, or exercise routine will solve emotional suffering. Body-focused work is essential, but like the self-help gurus who only focus on thought, wellness gurus tend to only focus on the body.

These promises create devastating expectations. When you believe that emotional transformation should happen quickly and easily, every technique that doesn't produce instant results feels like proof that you're broken or doing something wrong.

But here's what the quick-fix culture doesn't tell you: **Lasting emotional transformation requires fundamental changes in how your nervous system responds to life.** These changes happen in your body, not just your mind, and they unfold over time through consistent practice, not through magic bullets.

The Cognitive Prison: Why Thinking Differently Isn't Enough

One of the most persistent myths in mental health is that emotional problems are primarily thinking problems. This leads to the well-intentioned but ultimately limiting advice to "change your thoughts, change your feelings."

While cognitive approaches can be helpful, they miss a crucial reality: **Depression, anxiety, and anger are embodied experiences that live in your nervous system, not just in your thoughts.**

Consider what actually happens in each emotional state:

Depression isn't just sad thoughts—it's a full-body collapse. Your nervous system downregulates, your posture changes, your breathing becomes shallow, and your entire physiology shifts into a state of conservation and withdrawal.

Anxiety isn't just worried thoughts—it's systemic activation. Your heart rate increases, your muscles tense, your breathing becomes rapid and shallow, and your entire system prepares for threats that may not exist.

Anger isn't just hostile thoughts—it's mobilized energy. Your jaw clenches, your hands form fists, heat rises through your body, and your system organizes for confrontation or defense.

These are neurophysiological states, not just mental phenomena. This is why trying to think your way out of them often fails—you're using mental tools to address body-based experiences.

The Reinforcement Cycle: How Each Emotion Feeds the Others

What makes the depression-anxiety-anger triad so persistent is how each emotional state reinforces the others, creating what I call "the reinforcement cycle," as follows:

Depression → Anxiety: When you're depressed, your energy is low and tasks feel overwhelming. This creates anxiety about your inability to function, which then deepens the depression because now you're not just sad—you're worried about being sad.

Anxiety → Anger: Chronic anxiety is exhausting and often involves feeling powerless against racing thoughts and physical symptoms. This powerlessness frequently transforms into anger—at yourself, at your circumstances, and at the anxiety itself.

Anger → Depression: Intense anger often leads to guilt, shame, or exhaustion, especially if you've been taught that anger is "bad" or dangerous. This guilt and exhaustion can quickly spiral into depression.

The cycle becomes self-perpetuating. Each emotional state creates conditions that trigger the others, and traditional approaches that focus on managing individual emotions miss this interconnected dynamic entirely.

The Relationship Spiral: How Isolation Deepens Suffering

Emotional suffering doesn't just affect your internal experience—it systematically damages your connections with others, creating another vicious cycle:

The Depression Effect: You withdraw from social activities because they feel pointless or overwhelming. Others may interpret this withdrawal as rejection or disinterest.

The Anxiety Effect: You avoid social situations because they trigger anxious thoughts or physical symptoms. This avoidance reinforces the belief that social connection is dangerous or too difficult.

The Anger Effect: You may lash out at loved ones or isolate to protect them from your anger. Either way, relationships become strained or distant.

The cruel irony is that human connection is one of our most powerful medicines for emotional healing, yet depression, anxiety, and anger systematically cut us off from this very resource. Your nervous system needs co-regulation—the calming presence of other regulated nervous systems—but these emotional states convince you that you're better off alone.

Factors Beyond Individual Control

Most approaches to emotional healing focus exclusively on what you can change as an individual—your thoughts, behaviors, and choices. While personal agency matters, this narrow focus ignores critical factors that contribute to emotional suffering:

Trauma and Nervous System Development: Early experiences of neglect, abuse, or instability can create lasting changes in how your nervous system processes safety and threat.

These aren't just memories to process—they're embodied patterns that shape your baseline emotional responses.

Cultural and Social Conditions: Systemic oppression, economic instability, social isolation, and cultural disconnection create chronic stress that significantly impacts emotional wellbeing. Individual solutions can't fully address collective problems.

Environmental and Physical Factors: Poor nutrition, environmental toxins, hormonal imbalances, and other physical factors can all contribute to emotional instability. Ignoring the body's role in emotional health limits healing potential.

Intergenerational Patterns: Emotional patterns are often passed down through families, not just through learned behaviors but through epigenetic changes that affect nervous system development across generations.

Acknowledging these factors isn't about creating excuses—it's about understanding the full picture so you can work with reality rather than against it.

Why Partial Solutions Create Deeper Despair

When you approach emotional healing with incomplete tools, you often experience what I call "the improvement-relapse cycle." There are seven elements:

1. **Initial Hope**: You discover a new technique or approach that seems promising.
2. **Partial Improvement**: You experience some relief, often in one area, while others remain problematic.

3. **Plateau or Relapse**: The technique stops working, or you revert to old patterns.

4. **Self-Blame**: You conclude that you failed or didn't try hard enough.

5. **Deepened Despair**: Your belief in the possibility of lasting change diminishes.

6. **Reduced Investment**: You approach the next solution with less hope and commitment.

7. **Decreased Effectiveness**: With lower expectations and investment, the next approach is even less likely to succeed.

This cycle explains why many people feel more hopeless after years of trying different approaches than they did when they first sought help. It's not that you're resistant to healing—it's that you've been working with incomplete tools.

Are You Recognizing These Patterns?

As you read this chapter, notice what resonates with your own experience. Perhaps you've encountered:

- The exhausting experience of managing three different emotional problems that seem to take turns overwhelming you.
- The frustration of finding techniques that help temporarily but don't create lasting change.
- The confusion of working on depression only to have anxiety spike, or managing anger only to sink into depression.

- The growing suspicion that you're somehow uniquely difficult to help or that emotional peace isn't possible for you.
- The isolation that comes from feeling like no one understands the complexity of what you're experiencing.

If these patterns feel familiar, I want you to understand something crucial: **These experiences don't mean you're broken or doing something wrong. They mean you've been trying to solve an integration problem with fragmentation tools.**

The Integration Alternative: A Different Path Forward

Here's the revolutionary news: **There is another way.** Instead of treating depression, anxiety, and anger as separate problems requiring separate solutions, you can learn to work with them as interconnected expressions of the same underlying need for mind-body integration.

This approach differs from conventional treatments in several fundamental ways:

Holistic Rather Than Fragmented: Instead of managing individual symptoms, you'll learn to address the root disconnection that creates all three emotional patterns.

Body-Based Rather Than Mind-Only: You'll work with the physical, neurological reality of these emotional states, not just their mental content.

Integration-Focused Rather Than Suppression-Focused: Instead of trying to eliminate difficult emotions, you'll learn to transform them into sources of information and energy.

Process-Oriented Rather Than Outcome-Obsessed: You'll develop a sustainable relationship with emotional experience rather than seeking a permanent "cure."

Connection-Building Rather Than Isolation-Reinforcing: You'll learn to maintain relationships and seek support throughout your healing journey instead of withdrawing until you're "better."

The Promise of Embodied Transformation

This isn't another promise of quick fixes or magical transformations. What I'm offering is something more realistic and ultimately more powerful: **the possibility of fundamentally changing your relationship with emotional experiences through embodied awareness and integration practices.**

You will learn to:

- Recognize the early physical signs of emotional states before they overwhelm you.
- Work with your nervous system's natural capacity for regulation and resilience.
- Transform stuck emotional patterns into flowing, adaptive responses.
- Maintain connection with others even during difficult emotional periods.
- Develop confidence in your ability to navigate life's inevitable challenges.

This transformation doesn't happen overnight. The neural pathways that create emotional suffering develop over time, and creating new patterns also takes time and consistent practice. But gradual, sustainable change is not only possible—it's happening for people every day.

Your Courage Is Your Foundation

Before we move forward into the practical work, I want you to acknowledge something important: **the fact that you're still seeking solutions despite past disappointments is evidence of remarkable courage and resilience.**

Every time you've tried a new approach, despite previous failures, you've demonstrated faith in your own capacity for healing. Every time you've picked yourself up after a relapse, you've shown strength that depression, anxiety, and anger want you to believe you don't possess.

That courage—however small it might feel right now—is the foundation upon which your transformation will be built. Not false optimism or magical thinking, but the quiet persistence that keeps you moving toward wholeness even when the path seems unclear.

In the next chapter, we'll begin the practical work of developing somatic awareness—learning to listen to your body's wisdom and recognizing the physical patterns that underlie emotional suffering. This isn't just another technique to add to your collection; it's the foundation for everything that follows.

Are you ready to stop fighting three separate wars and start healing one integrated system? If so, let's continue this journey together, moving from fragmentation toward wholeness, from resistance toward integration, and from suffering toward transformation.

Chapter 3

The 8-Week Protocol for Emotional Transformation

Despite everything that makes emotional suffering feel so persistent and overwhelming, profound transformation truly is possible. I've witnessed it countless times—people who felt trapped in cycles of depression, anxiety, and anger discovering that these weren't separate enemies to battle but interconnected expressions of one fundamental disconnection that could be healed.

The path to this transformation isn't always linear or easy, but it exists, and it's available to you. What makes the difference isn't finding the perfect technique or having extraordinary willpower—it's understanding that **lasting emotional healing happens through mind-body integration**, addressing your whole being rather than just isolated symptoms.

Research supports this integrated approach. A comprehensive 2022 meta-analysis of emotional regulation interventions found that approaches combining somatic awareness, cognitive flexibility, relational healing, and meaning-making led to significantly better outcomes than single-method treatments. This holds true even for people who've struggled with emotional patterns for decades or haven't responded to traditional approaches in the past.

My own journey mirrors these findings. The most profound transformations I've witnessed—and experienced personally—occur when people learn to work with their emotions as embodied experiences, recognizing that depression, anxiety, and anger are all expressions of the same underlying need for integration and wholeness.

The Revolutionary Understanding: One System, One Solution

Traditional approaches treat depression, anxiety, and anger as separate disorders requiring separate interventions. This fragmented perspective keeps people cycling through partial solutions—managing depression one week, coping with anxiety the next, controlling anger after that—without ever addressing the root cause.

This protocol is different. It's based on a revolutionary understanding: **Depression, anxiety, and anger are different expressions of the same mind-body disconnection.** When you heal this fundamental split, all three emotional patterns begin to transform naturally.

Think of it this way: instead of learning three different languages to communicate with three different aspects of yourself, you'll learn one unified language—the language of embodied awareness—that allows you to work with your entire emotional system as an integrated whole.

The 8-Week Transformation Protocol: Your Journey to Integration

This isn't another collection of coping strategies or management techniques. This is a comprehensive protocol for fundamental transformation—changing not just how you think about emotions but how you experience them in your body, express them in relationships, and integrate them into a meaningful life.

Each week builds on the previous one, creating a spiral of healing that addresses different dimensions of your experience while strengthening the foundation of mind-body integration. By the end of eight weeks, you'll have developed what I call "embodied emotional intelligence"—the ability to work with all your emotions as allies rather than enemies.

Week 1

Developing Somatic Awareness: The Foundation of Integration

Your emotional patterns live in your body. Depression shows up as collapsed posture, shallow breathing, and muscular withdrawal. Anxiety manifests as tension, activation, and restless energy. Anger appears as clenched muscles, heat, and mobilized force.

The first week focuses on developing **somatic awareness**—the ability to recognize how emotions manifest physically before they overwhelm your conscious mind. This isn't just body scanning or relaxation techniques; it's learning to read the language your nervous system speaks through sensation.

You'll practice:

- **Foundation Grounding**: Establishing safety and presence in your body.
- **Sensation Tracking**: Learning to identify and describe physical sensations without judgment.
- **Early Warning Recognition**: Detecting the physical signs of emotional shifts before they become overwhelming.
- **Basic Regulation**: Simple techniques for returning to baseline when emotions spike.

Many people have learned to disconnect from their bodies as protection against pain or trauma. Week 1 gently guides you back into a relationship with your physical self, creating the foundation for all the work that follows.

Week 2

Nervous System Regulation: Building Your Internal Resources

Emotional suffering often reflects nervous system dysregulation—being stuck in states of collapse (depression), hyperactivation (anxiety), or defensive mobilization (anger). Week 2 teaches you to work directly with your nervous system's natural capacity for regulation and resilience.

Your nervous system isn't fixed or broken—it's highly responsive to intentional practices. Through specific somatic techniques, you'll learn to shift from states of dysregulation into what's called "the window of tolerance"—a state where you can feel emotions without being overwhelmed by them.

Key practices include:

- **Pendulation**: Moving attention between areas of comfort and discomfort to build resilience.
- **Resourcing**: Identifying and strengthening your body's natural sources of calm and strength.
- **Boundary Work**: Using physical awareness to set emotional and energetic boundaries.
- **Co-Regulation Skills**: Learning to use relationships and your environment to support nervous system balance.

This week isn't about eliminating difficult emotions but about creating a stable internal foundation that can hold the full spectrum of emotional experience.

Week 3

Emotional Integration: Transforming Your Relationship with Feeling

Most approaches to emotional healing focus on managing or controlling difficult feelings. This protocol takes a radically different approach: **learning to work with emotions as embodied messengers carrying important information about your needs, boundaries, and authentic self.**

Depression often carries messages about the need for rest, grieving, or life changes. Anxiety frequently signals unmet needs for safety, preparation, or boundary-setting. Anger typically communicates violations of values, the need for protection, or calls to authentic action.

Week 3 practices include:

- **Emotional Mapping**: Learning to track how different emotions show up in your unique body.

- **Message Translation**: Understanding what your emotions are trying to communicate.
- **Integration Techniques**: Working with stuck emotional patterns through somatic approaches.
- **Alchemy Practices**: Transforming emotional energy into fuel for positive change.

Instead of fighting your emotions, you'll learn to dance with them, using their energy and information to create more authentic, fulfilling ways of being.

Week 4

Somatic Cognitive Integration: Bridging Body and Mind

Traditional cognitive approaches try to change emotions by changing thoughts. This protocol recognizes that **lasting cognitive change must include the body**—that thoughts and physical states are inseparable aspects of one integrated system.

Depression, anxiety, and anger all involve both mental patterns and physical states. Real transformation happens when you learn to work with both dimensions simultaneously, using body awareness to support mental flexibility and mental clarity to guide physical regulation.

This week's practices consist of:

- **Thought-Body Tracking**: Recognizing how different thought patterns show up physically.
- **Somatic Cognitive Restructuring**: Using body-based techniques to create new mental patterns.
- **Integration Exercises**: Practices that work with thoughts and sensations as one unified experience.

- **Pattern Interruption:** Using physical shifts to interrupt stuck mental loops.

You'll discover that changing your relationship with your body naturally shifts your mental patterns, and developing cognitive flexibility supports greater somatic awareness.

Week 5

Relational Healing: Connection as Medicine

Emotional patterns both affect and are affected by relationships. Depression, anxiety, and anger can create isolation, codependency, or conflict that reinforces the very patterns you're trying to change. Week 5 focuses on healing relationship dynamics that maintain emotional suffering.

Many people develop relationship patterns that made sense given past experiences but ultimately reinforce disconnection and pain. These might include emotional withdrawal, people-pleasing, boundary violations, or conflict avoidance—all attempts at protection that ultimately create more isolation.

Key areas of focus include:

- **Attachment Pattern Recognition:** Understanding how early relationships shaped your emotional patterns.
- **Authentic Expression:** Learning to share your true feelings and needs without overwhelming others.
- **Boundary Intelligence:** Using body awareness to set and maintain healthy relational boundaries.
- **Co-regulation Skills:** Developing relationships that support rather than trigger dysregulation.

This isn't about fixing relationships or finding perfect people to connect with—it's about developing the capacity for authentic connection that supports your ongoing emotional integration.

Week 6

Meaning and Purpose Integration: Connecting to Something Larger

Emotional suffering often involves disconnection from meaning and purpose. Depression can make everything feel pointless. Anxiety can make it impossible to focus on what matters. Anger can consume energy that might otherwise flow toward meaningful activity.

Week 6 explores how to reconnect with what gives your life meaning, even in small ways. This isn't about finding one grand purpose but about developing what researchers call "eudaimonic well-being"—the sense that your life has meaning, direction, and authentic expression.

Practices include:

- **Values Embodiment**: Connecting to your deepest values through somatic awareness.
- **Purpose Practices**: Small, meaningful actions that align with your authentic self.
- **Service Integration**: Contributing to something larger than yourself in ways that honor your unique gifts.
- **Spiritual Somatic Practices**: Connecting to the sacred through embodied experience.

Research consistently shows that meaning-centered approaches significantly reduce symptoms of depression, anxiety, and anger, especially when combined with somatic and relational work.

Week 7

Integration and Daily Practice: Making Transformation Sustainable

All the insights and skills in the world won't create lasting change if they aren't woven into the fabric of daily life. Week 7 focuses on creating sustainable practices that support ongoing integration and prevent relapse into old patterns.

Most people make the mistake of trying to change too much too quickly, leading to overwhelm and the abandonment of new practices. Instead, you'll learn to build personalized daily rhythms that incorporate small but powerful integration practices fitting your specific needs and circumstances.

This consists of:

- **Morning Integration Practices**: Starting each day with embodied awareness and intention.
- **Midday Reset Techniques**: Maintaining integration during busy or challenging periods.
- **Evening Integration**: Processing the day's experiences and preparing for restorative rest.
- **Crisis Navigation**: Tools for maintaining integration during particularly difficult periods.

These aren't rigid "should do" lists but flexible frameworks that honor both your healing needs and real-life constraints. The goal is consistency over perfection, creating gentle habits that gradually reshape your experience from the inside out.

Week 8

Embodied Resilience: Thriving Through Life's Challenges

Emotional transformation isn't a destination but an ongoing journey of deepening integration. There will be challenges, setbacks, and difficult periods even as overall well-being improves. Week 8 focuses on building what I call "embodied resilience"—the capacity to navigate life's inevitable difficulties while maintaining connection to your integrated self.

Resilience isn't about never struggling; it's about having the tools to move through struggles without losing touch with your body's wisdom, your emotional intelligence, your relational capacity, and your sense of meaning.

Final integration incorporates:

- **Early Warning Systems**: Recognizing when old patterns are trying to reassert themselves.
- **Intervention Strategies**: Effective tools for redirecting dysregulation before it becomes overwhelming.
- **Support Network Development**: Creating relationships that support your ongoing integration.
- **Continuous Growth Planning**: Setting intentions for deepening transformation beyond the eight weeks.

This final week also focuses on celebrating your progress, acknowledging how much you've grown, and preparing for the lifelong journey of embodied emotional intelligence.

Your Unique Path Through Integration

These eight weeks offer a comprehensive protocol for emotional transformation—addressing your whole being rather than isolated symptoms. Each week builds on the previous ones, creating a foundation for lasting change that honors the complexity of your experience while providing practical, actionable tools.

As we explore each week in detail throughout the following chapters, you'll receive specific practices, reflection exercises, and guidance for implementing these principles in your daily life. Some practices will resonate immediately; others might feel challenging at first. This is normal and expected. The key is approaching this journey with curiosity and self-compassion rather than rigid expectations.

Honoring Your Own Timing

While this system is structured as an eight-week journey, honor your own timing and needs. Some people move through quickly, experiencing rapid shifts and integration. Others need more time to develop each skill before moving forward. Both approaches are valid.

There's wisdom in an old saying: "The stream said to the river, 'You go quickly, I go slowly; together we reach the sea.'" The eight-week structure provides guidance and momentum, but let your own inner wisdom determine your pace.

Additionally, this method contains far more practices and insights than can be fully integrated in one eight-week cycle. My intention is that you'll find the most beneficial approaches for your initial transformation, then return to deepen your practice, explore new techniques, and expand your repertoire of integration skills.

Many people find that cycling through the protocol multiple times—each cycle deeper and more nuanced than the last—creates profound and lasting transformation.

The Promise of Integration

This isn't a promise of overnight transformation or a life free from emotional challenges. What I'm offering is something more realistic and ultimately more powerful: **the possibility of fundamentally changing your relationship with emotional experience through embodied integration.**

You will learn to:

- Experience depression, anxiety, and anger as temporary states rather than fixed identities.
- Work with difficult emotions as sources of information and energy rather than overwhelming threats.
- Maintain a connection to your body's wisdom even during challenging periods.
- Create relationships that support rather than trigger emotional dysregulation.
- Find meaning and purpose that sustain you through life's inevitable difficulties.

This transformation happens gradually, through consistent practice and gentle persistence. Small changes accumulate into profound shifts when supported by an integrated approach that honors both your humanity and your capacity for growth.

Your Journey Begins with One Breath

Before we dive into the specific practices of Week 1, take a moment to acknowledge the courage it requires to begin this journey. Every time you've sought healing despite past disappointments, you've demonstrated remarkable resilience and faith in your own capacity for transformation.

That faith—however small it might feel right now—is the seed from which your integration will grow. Not through magical thinking or forcing change, but through patient, consistent practice of becoming more fully yourself.

Are you ready to begin this journey toward embodied emotional intelligence? Not with false promises of perfection, but with real tools that can create lasting transformation when practiced with dedication and self-compassion?

If so, let's begin. Week 1 awaits—your first step toward integrating the wisdom of your body, the intelligence of your emotions, and the fullness of your authentic self.

Chapter 4

Week 1: Developing Somatic Awareness—The Foundation of Integration

The Body Knows Before the Mind Understands

At 48, Michael sat in his empty apartment staring at the final child support payment confirmation on his phone screen. After three divorces and eighteen years of payments, he was finally free—yet he had never felt more trapped. The silence in his one-bedroom rental felt deafening. His chest was tight, his shoulders had crept up toward his ears, and there was a constant knot in his stomach that he'd been carrying for months.

"I should be relieved," he told himself. "I should be excited about having money for myself again." But instead of relief, waves of panic would wash over him at random moments. He'd catch himself holding his breath, his jaw clenched so tight it ached. At night, he'd lie awake with his heart racing, thinking about his retirement account that barely existed, his dating life that felt hopeless, and the growing certainty that he was a complete failure at life.

What Michael didn't understand was that his body was speaking to him in a language he'd never learned to interpret. The tightness in his chest wasn't just stress—it was anxiety preparing his system for threats that existed more in his imagination than reality. The collapsed feeling in his shoulders wasn't just fatigue—it was his nervous system expressing the depression that came with years of feeling defeated. The clenched jaw wasn't just tension—it was anger at himself, at his choices, at the life he'd somehow created.

Michael's body was carrying the full weight of his emotional experience, but like most of us, he'd learned to ignore these physical signals until they became overwhelming. He lived primarily in his head, analyzing his problems, judging his choices, and planning and worrying about the future. Meanwhile, his body—the very foundation of his emotional experience—remained a stranger to him.

Have You Lost Touch With Your Body's Wisdom?

As you read Michael's story, I wonder if you recognize something familiar. Perhaps you too have noticed that your emotional struggles seem to live not just in your thoughts but in your physical being. Maybe you've experienced:

- The heavy feeling in your chest when depression settles in.
- The racing heart and tight muscles that accompany anxiety.
- The clenched jaw or burning sensation that signals rising anger.

- The chronic tension that never seems to fully release.
- The exhaustion that goes deeper than just needing sleep.
- The sense of being disconnected from your own body, living primarily "in your head."

If these experiences resonate, you're discovering something profound: **Your emotions are not just mental experiences—they are full-body phenomena.** Depression, anxiety, and anger don't just happen in your brain; they happen in your nervous system, your muscles, your breathing, your posture, and every cell of your being.

This understanding changes everything about how healing becomes possible. Instead of trying to think your way out of emotional patterns, you can learn to work directly with the physical manifestations of these states. Instead of being surprised by emotional overwhelm, you can develop the ability to recognize and respond to early physical warning signs.

The Language Your Body Speaks

Your nervous system is constantly communicating with you through physical sensations, but most of us have never learned to understand this language. We live in a culture that prioritizes mental analysis over bodily awareness, thinking over feeling, and doing over being. As a result, we become disconnected from one of our most important sources of information and healing capacity.

Consider what research tells us about the body-emotion connection: when you feel depressed, your posture literally changes—your shoulders round forward, your head drops, and your breathing becomes shallow. When anxiety spikes, your muscles tense, your heart rate increases, and your entire system mobilizes for action. When anger arises, your jaw clenches, your hands form fists, and heat rises through your body.

These aren't just side effects of emotional states—they are integral parts of how emotions exist in your system. Physical patterns and emotional experiences are so intertwined that changing one directly impacts the other. This is why developing somatic awareness—the ability to sense and work with your body's signals—is the absolute foundation of emotional transformation.

Michael's Journey Into Body Awareness

When Michael first began practicing somatic awareness, he was skeptical. "How is paying attention to my body going to help with my financial anxiety or my loneliness?" he asked. But he was desperate enough to try anything.

His first assignment was simple: three times a day, stop whatever he was doing and spend two minutes noticing what was happening in his body. Not trying to change anything, not judging what he found, just noticing.

The first week was revelatory. Michael discovered that his anxiety had a very specific physical signature; it started with a slight tightening around his heart, moved up into his throat as a choking sensation, and then spread through his arms as restless energy that made him want to pace or fidget. His depression showed up differently—as a heavy, sinking feeling in his chest and belly, accompanied by the sensation that his whole body was deflating.

Most surprisingly, he began to notice these physical changes before his mind registered the emotional shift. His body was giving him early warning signals—information he could use to respond to emotional states before they became overwhelming.

By the third week of his practice, Michael had made a crucial discovery. He was checking his email inbox when he felt that familiar tightening around his heart. Instead of letting it build into full anxiety, he paused. He took three slow breaths, allowing his belly to expand. He gently moved his shoulders away from his ears. The anxious spiral that usually would have consumed the next hour simply... didn't happen.

"It was like I caught the wave before it could crash over me," he explained. "For the first time in years, I felt like I had some choice in how I responded to my emotions."

The Four Foundations of Somatic Awareness

Based on research in neuroscience, trauma therapy, and somatic psychology, I've identified four essential foundations for developing body awareness that supports emotional integration:

1. Foundation Grounding: Creating Safety in Your Body

Before you can explore difficult emotions, your nervous system needs to know it's safe to feel. Grounding practices help you establish a sense of stability and presence in your physical being.

The Practice: Sit comfortably with your feet on the floor. Feel the weight of your body in the chair and your feet making contact with the ground. Notice that in this moment, you are supported. Breathe naturally and let yourself settle into this sense of being held by the earth. Practice this for 2–3 minutes several times daily.

Why It Works: Grounding activates your parasympathetic nervous system—the part responsible for rest, digestion, and healing. When this system is engaged, your body feels safe enough to process and integrate emotional experiences.

2. Sensation Tracking: Learning Your Body's Language

Most people describe their physical experience in very general terms: "tense," "tired," and "stressed." Developing somatic awareness requires becoming much more specific and nuanced in how you sense and describe bodily sensations.

The Practice: Throughout the day, pause and scan your body from head to toe. Instead of judging sensations as "good" or "bad," describe them simply: "There's a tight band around my forehead. My jaw feels clenched. There's a flutter in my stomach. My shoulders are lifted toward my ears." Practice this without trying to change anything.

Why It Works: The more precisely you can identify physical sensations, the more information you have about your emotional state. This awareness allows you to respond skillfully rather than react automatically.

3. Early Warning Recognition: Catching Emotions as They Arise

Each emotional state has physical precursors—subtle bodily changes that occur before the full emotional experience takes hold. Learning to recognize these early warning signs gives you the opportunity to work with emotions before they become overwhelming.

The Practice: Begin mapping your personal emotional signatures. Notice what depression feels like in its earliest stages: perhaps a slight heaviness in your chest or a subtle slowing of your movements. Track anxiety's first signals: maybe a flutter in your stomach or a quickening of your breath. Observe anger's initial manifestation: possibly tension in your jaw or heat beginning to rise from your body.

Why It Works: Early intervention is far more effective than crisis management. When you can sense emotional shifts as they begin, you can use somatic techniques to guide your nervous system toward regulation rather than dysregulation.

4. Basic Regulation: Simple Tools for Returning to Balance

Once you can recognize when your nervous system is moving toward dysregulation, you need simple, effective tools for returning to a state of balance and presence.

The Practice: Develop a tool kit of go-to regulation techniques:

- **Conscious breathing**: Slow, deep breaths that emphasize a longer exhale than inhale.
- **Progressive muscle relaxation**: Deliberately tensing and then releasing different muscle groups.
- **Gentle movement**: Stretching, walking, or other movement that helps release stuck energy.
- **Self-touch**: Placing your hand on your heart or giving yourself a gentle hug.

Why It Works: These practices directly influence your autonomic nervous system, helping shift you from states of fight/flight (anxiety) or freeze (depression) back into social engagement and presence.

Applying Somatic Awareness to Michael's Story

Looking back at Michael's situation, imagine how different his experience might have been if he had possessed these somatic awareness skills from the beginning.

Instead of being blindsided by anxiety attacks, he would have noticed the early tightening around his heart and used conscious breathing to prevent escalation. Rather than sinking into depressive spirals about his failures, he would have recognized the heavy, collapsing sensation in his chest and used grounding techniques to maintain his sense of stability and possibility.

Most importantly, instead of living primarily in his worried thoughts about the future, he would have developed the capacity to stay present in his body, connected to his actual experience in each moment rather than lost in catastrophic thinking.

The financial stress wouldn't have disappeared, but his relationship to that stress would have been fundamentally different. Instead of being overwhelmed by it, he could have worked with it as information about what needed attention, rather than evidence of his inadequacy.

Your Body as Your Greatest Ally

Perhaps the most radical shift that comes with developing somatic awareness is recognizing your body not as the source of your problems, but as your greatest ally in healing them. Your body is not betraying you when it feels anxious, depressed, or angry—it's trying to communicate with you.

Depression's physical heaviness might be your nervous system's way of slowing you down, insisting you take time to process grief or make necessary life changes. Anxiety's activation might be your body's attempt to mobilize you toward action or alert you to something requiring attention. Anger's heat and energy might be your system's way of protecting your boundaries or motivating you to advocate for your values.

When you learn to listen to these physical messages with curiosity rather than judgment, you gain access to a vast source of wisdom that can guide your choices and support your healing.

Starting Your Own Somatic Awareness Practice

Beginning to develop somatic awareness doesn't require hours of meditation or complex techniques. It starts with simple, consistent attention to your physical experience throughout the day.

Week 1 Daily Practice:

1. **Morning Grounding** (5 minutes): Upon waking, before getting out of bed, spend a few minutes feeling the weight of your body and setting an intention to stay connected to physical sensations throughout the day.

2. **Midday Check-ins** (2 minutes, 3 times): Set reminders to pause and scan your body. Notice what you're carrying physically and breathe into any areas of tension or discomfort.

3. **Evening Integration** (10 minutes): Before sleep, review the day's emotional experiences and their physical manifestations. Notice patterns and acknowledge your body's wisdom in communicating with you.

4. **Sensation Journaling**: Keep brief notes about the connections you notice between physical sensations and emotional states. This helps you develop your personal emotional-physical map.

The Promise of Embodied Awareness

Developing somatic awareness won't eliminate difficult emotions from your life—nor should it. What it will do is fundamentally change your relationship with these emotions, transforming them from overwhelming threats into manageable experiences that carry valuable information.

As you develop the ability to stay present with your physical experience, you'll discover that emotions have natural rhythms—they arise, peak, and naturally resolve when not resisted or amplified by mental stories. You'll find that your body has an innate capacity for regulation and healing that becomes available when you learn to work with it rather than against it.

Most importantly, you'll begin to experience yourself as an integrated being—not a mind trying to control a body, but a unified system where physical awareness supports emotional wisdom, and emotional intelligence guides physical well-being.

This is the foundation on which all lasting emotional transformation is built. In the coming weeks, we'll build on this somatic awareness to develop increasingly sophisticated skills for working with depression, anxiety, and anger as allies in your journey toward wholeness.

But it all begins here, with this simple but profound practice: learning to come home to your body, to listen to its signals, and to trust its wisdom. Your body has been waiting patiently for you to remember this connection. It's time to begin.

Your Week 1 Action Plan: The Somatic Awareness Implementation Guide

Knowledge without action remains merely information. To transform your relationship with emotions through somatic awareness, you need a clear, practical implementation strategy. This week's action plan will guide you step-by-step through establishing a sustainable practice that builds the foundation for everything that follows.

Day 1–2: Establishing Your Baseline

Morning Ritual: Before getting out of bed, spend five minutes conducting a full-body scan. Starting from the top of your head, slowly move your attention down through your body, noticing any sensations without trying to change them. Simply observe tension, relaxation, warmth, coolness, heaviness, lightness, pain, and comfort. Create a mental snapshot of your "baseline" physical state.

Evening Documentation: Before sleep, spend ten minutes writing in a journal specifically about physical sensations you noticed throughout the day. Use descriptive language rather than judgmental terms. Instead of "I felt terrible," write "There was a tight band around my forehead, my shoulders felt pulled up toward my ears, and there was a churning sensation in my stomach."

Key Goal: Develop your vocabulary for physical sensations and begin noticing patterns in how emotions show up in your body.

Day 3–4: Tracking Emotional-Physical Connections

Hourly Check-ins: Set eight alarms throughout your waking hours. When the alarm sounds, pause whatever you're doing and ask, "What am I feeling emotionally right now?" Then immediately ask, "How is this showing up in my body?" Write down both the emotion and its physical manifestation.

Emotion-Body Mapping: Create three columns in your journal: "Emotion," "Physical Sensation," and "Location in Body." Begin mapping your unique patterns. You might discover that anxiety starts as a flutter in your chest, depression feels like heaviness in your limbs, or anger manifests as heat rising from your belly.

Key Goal: Develop awareness of the connection between your emotional states and their physical expressions.

Day 5–6: Early Warning System Development

Pre-Overwhelm Tracking: Focus specifically on catching emotional states before they become overwhelming. Pay particular attention to subtle physical changes that occur before you feel emotionally activated. This might be a slight quickening of breath before anxiety, a gentle sinking feeling before sadness, or a tiny jaw clench before irritation.

Intervention Practice: When you notice early physical warning signs, implement one of these immediate responses:

- Take five slow, deep breaths with longer exhales than inhales.
- Gently move your shoulders away from your ears and soften your jaw.
- Place one hand on your heart and one on your belly, breathing into both.
- Take a brief walk or do gentle stretching.

Key Goal: Develop the ability to recognize and respond to emotional states before they become overwhelming.

Day 7: Integration and Planning

Weekly Review: Look back through your week's documentation. What patterns do you notice? Which physical sensations consistently accompany which emotions? What early warning signs are most reliable for you? Which intervention techniques were most effective?

Personalized Protocol Creation: Based on your week's observations, create your personalized "Emotional Early Warning and Response System." This should include:

- Your top three most reliable physical warning signs for each emotion (depression, anxiety, anger).
- Your three most effective regulation techniques.
- Your optimal timing for check-ins based on your daily schedule.

Key Goal: Establish a sustainable, personalized practice for ongoing somatic awareness development.

Weekly Success Metrics

By the end of Week 1, you should be able to:

- Identify at least five specific physical sensations that accompany your emotional states.
- Recognize at least one early physical warning sign for each major emotion.
- Successfully use at least one somatic regulation technique to shift your state.
- Maintain consistent daily check-ins with your body.

Troubleshooting Common Challenges

"I can't feel anything." If you have difficulty sensing physical sensations, start with obvious ones: the feeling of your clothes against your skin, the temperature of the air, and the weight of your body in a chair. Gradually work toward more subtle sensations.

"It feels overwhelming to pay attention to my body." This is common, especially if you've experienced trauma. Go slowly. Start with just thirty seconds of body awareness at a time. Focus on areas that feel safe and comfortable before exploring more challenging sensations.

"I keep forgetting to check in." Use technology to support your practice. Set phone alarms with labels like "Body Check" or "How am I feeling physically?" Place sticky notes in visible locations as reminders.

"I don't have time." The practices this week require less than thirty minutes total per day. Remember that developing somatic awareness will ultimately save you time by preventing emotional overwhelm and improving your ability to self-regulate.

Guided Somatic Integration Session: Coming Home to Your Body

Note: This session can be read silently to yourself, recorded in your own voice, or used as a guide for your own meditation practice. Allow approximately 20–25 minutes for the complete experience.

Find a comfortable position where you can remain alert yet relaxed. This might be sitting in a chair with your feet on the ground, lying down with a pillow under your knees, or any position that feels supportive for your body right now. There's no perfect way to do this—only what works for you in this moment.

Allow your eyes to close or soften your gaze downward, whatever feels most natural. Take a moment to notice that you've chosen to give yourself this time, this space for healing and integration. This choice itself is an act of self-care, a recognition that your relationship with your body matters.

Begin by simply noticing that you are breathing. You don't need to change your breath—just observe it. Notice how you are breathing and that it is happening without any effort or control on your part. Your body knows exactly how to breathe, how to nourish itself, and how to sustain life moment by moment. This is your body's wisdom at work.

Now, let your attention settle into the places where your body makes contact with support. Feel the weight of your body being held—by the chair, by the floor, by the earth itself. You are supported right now. You are held. Let yourself sink into this support, allowing your body to release any unnecessary tension, anything holding on that no longer serves you.

Notice your feet. If they're touching the ground, feel that connection. If they're resting on a surface, notice that support. Your feet carry you through life, connecting you to the earth with each step. Send a gentle appreciation to your feet for all they do, for how they support you, ground you, and help you move through the world.

Let your attention move up into your legs. Notice your calves, your shins, your knees, your thighs. These strong muscles and bones that carry you, that help you stand, walk, and run when needed. You might notice areas of tension or holding on in your legs. If you do, simply acknowledge them with kindness. Send your breath to any areas that feel tight or stressed, not trying to force them to relax, but offering them the nourishment of your attention and breath.

Bring your awareness to your pelvis and lower back. This is the base of your spine, your center of gravity, your foundation. Notice how this area of your body works to keep you upright and to provide stability and support. If there's tension here, remember that tension often represents your body's attempt to provide support and protection. Thank your lower back for working so hard to support you.

Let your attention rise to your belly, that soft, vulnerable space that often holds so much emotion. Place one hand gently on your belly if that feels comfortable. Notice how your belly rises and falls with each breath. This is where your body processes emotions, where you literally digest your experiences. Send appreciation to your belly for its role in helping you process life's experiences.

Move your awareness to your chest, your heart space. Place your other hand here if you'd like. Notice the rhythm of your heartbeat, that constant, faithful pulse that has been with you since before you were born and will be with you until your last moment. Your heart beats approximately 100,000 times each day, pumping life through your entire system. Take a moment to marvel at this incredible organ that works tirelessly to sustain you.

Notice your shoulders. These often carry the weight of the world. If your shoulders are pulled up toward your ears, simply notice this without judgment. Your shoulders might be holding tension from stress, responsibility, or the unconscious effort to protect your heart. Breathe into your shoulders, offering them permission to soften, to release, to let go of any burden they don't need to carry right now.

Bring your attention to your arms, these extensions of your heart that allow you to reach out, to embrace, to create, and to express. Notice your hands, these incredible instruments that can create art, offer comfort, and express love through touch. Your hands carry so much wisdom—they know how to soothe a crying child, how to create beauty, and how to offer healing touch to yourself and others.

Let your awareness move to your neck and throat, that bridge between your mind and body, the place where your voice originates. Your throat is the gateway for your authentic expression, the place where your inner truth becomes your external voice. If there's tension in your throat, this might be unexpressed emotions, unspoken truths, or the effort to keep feelings inside. Breathe gently into your throat, offering it space to open, to soften.

Notice your jaw, this powerful muscle that works constantly—speaking, eating, sometimes clenching with stress or determination. If your jaw is tight, simply acknowledge this holding on. Your jaw might be working to keep emotions contained, to maintain control, or to power through difficult experiences. Send your jaw appreciation for its strength and offer it permission to soften.

Bring your attention to your face, this expressive canvas that communicates so much to the world. Notice your eyes, your cheeks, your forehead. If there's tension in your face, remember that your facial muscles often mirror your emotional state. Send gentleness to your face, allowing it to soften into its natural, relaxed expression.

Finally, notice your head, your brain, this incredible organ that processes thousands of thoughts each day, that works constantly to make sense of your experience, to keep you safe, and to help you navigate life. Thank your brain for all its hard work, and offer it permission to rest, to simply be present with your body rather than analyzing or figuring out.

Now, take a moment to sense your body as a complete, integrated system. From the top of your head to the tips of your toes, you are one unified being. Your emotions don't live only in your mind—they live in every cell, every muscle, every organ. Your body is not just a vehicle for your consciousness—it is an integral part of who you are.

Notice if there are any areas of your body that feel particularly tense or uncomfortable or are calling for attention. Rather than trying to fix or change these sensations, simply place your breath and your kind attention there. Imagine breathing directly into these areas, offering them the nourishment of oxygen and the medicine of your presence.

If you're noticing emotions arising during this body scan—perhaps sadness, anxiety, anger, or even joy—welcome them. These emotions are information from your body's wisdom. They're not problems to be solved but experiences to be acknowledged. Your body is speaking to you through these feelings, offering you important information about your needs, your boundaries, and your authentic self.

Take a moment to ask your body, "What do you need right now?" Don't force an answer, but simply listen with curiosity.

Your body might need rest, movement, nourishment, touch, or simply continued presence and attention. Whatever arises, receive it without judgment.

Now, imagine that with each breath, you're strengthening the connection between your conscious awareness and your body's wisdom. With each inhale, you're drawing in presence, awareness, and integration. With each exhale, you're releasing disconnection, tension, and the habit of living only in your head.

Set an intention to carry this body awareness with you as you return to your daily life. Remember that your body is always with you, always available as a source of information, wisdom, and grounding. Throughout your day, you can return to this sense of embodied presence simply by taking a breath and asking, "What is my body telling me right now?"

When you're ready, begin to bring gentle movement back into your body. Wiggle your fingers and toes. Take a deeper breath. If your eyes are closed, slowly open them. Take a moment before you stand up to appreciate this time you've given yourself, this opportunity to come home to your body.

Remember, this practice of somatic awareness is not about achieving a particular state or feeling. It's about developing a relationship with your body based on curiosity, kindness, and respect. Your body has been with you through every experience of your life, and it will continue to be your partner in healing and growth.

Each time you practice this kind of embodied awareness, you're strengthening the foundation for emotional integration. You're learning to recognize emotions not as overwhelming forces that happen to you, but as embodied experiences that you can sense, understand, and work with skillfully.

This is the beginning of a profound transformation—not just in how you manage difficult emotions, but in how you experience being fully, authentically, integrally yourself.

Chapter 5

Week 2: Nervous System Regulation—Building Your Internal Resources

When Your Body's Alarm System Gets Stuck

Rebecca had always been what others called "high-functioning." At 52, she managed a demanding career in healthcare administration, maintained a spotless home, and never missed her mother's weekly doctor appointments. But lately, something had shifted. Her body felt like it was running on a motor that wouldn't turn off.

Even during quiet moments—watching TV, lying in bed, sitting at her desk—her heart would race for no apparent reason. Her muscles stayed perpetually tense, as if braced for an emergency that never came. Sleep became elusive; her mind would quiet, but her body remained vigilant, alert, and activated. She'd wake up exhausted, as if she'd been running marathons in her sleep.

"I feel like I'm living in fight-or-flight mode 24/7," she told her doctor, who suggested it was just stress and recommended she try to relax more. But Rebecca had tried everything—yoga classes, meditation apps, warm baths, and chamomile tea. Nothing seemed to touch the deep activation thrumming through her nervous system.

What Rebecca didn't understand was that her nervous system wasn't broken—it was stuck. Years of caring for others while ignoring her own needs, of pushing through exhaustion and overwhelm, and of living in chronic low-level stress had dysregulated her autonomic nervous system. Her body's natural alarm system, designed to activate temporarily in response to actual threats, had become chronically engaged.

Rebecca was living outside what trauma therapists call "the window of tolerance"—that optimal zone where you can experience emotions, stress, and challenges without becoming overwhelmed or shutting down. Instead, she was trapped in hyperactivation, her nervous system stuck in a state of constant mobilization even when no real danger existed.

Understanding Your Nervous System's Three States

Your autonomic nervous system, the part that controls functions like heartbeat, breathing, and digestion, operates in three primary states that directly impact your emotional experience:

Social Engagement (Window of Tolerance): This is your optimal state—calm but alert, able to connect with others, process emotions, and respond to challenges without becoming overwhelmed. In this state, you feel safe, present, and capable.

Sympathetic Activation (Fight/Flight): When your system perceives a threat, it mobilizes energy for action. Heart rate increases, muscles tense, and breathing quickens. This state is essential for handling real dangers but becomes problematic when chronically activated by modern stressors, relationship conflicts, or traumatic memories. This is often experienced as anxiety, panic, anger, or restless agitation.

Dorsal Shutdown (Freeze/Collapse): When threats feel overwhelming or inescapable, your system may shift into protective shutdown. Energy drops, you feel disconnected or numb, and motivation disappears. This state helped our ancestors survive by "playing dead," but in modern life, it often manifests as depression, dissociation, or profound fatigue.

Understanding these states changes everything about how you relate to your emotional experiences. Depression isn't a character flaw—it's often your nervous system stuck in dorsal shutdown. Anxiety isn't weakness—it's sympathetic activation triggered by perceived threats. Anger isn't just an emotion—it's mobilized energy preparing your system for action.

Are You Living Outside Your Window of Tolerance?

As you consider Rebecca's experience, reflect on your own nervous system patterns. Perhaps you recognize the following:

Signs of Chronic Hyperactivation (Stuck in Fight/Flight):

- Racing thoughts that won't quiet down.
- Physical tension that never fully releases.
- Hypervigilance—constantly scanning for problems or threats.
- Difficulty sleeping or staying asleep.
- Feeling wired but tired.
- Irritability or anger that seems disproportionate to situations.

- Difficulty sitting still or relaxing.

Signs of Chronic Shutdown (Stuck in Freeze/Collapse):

- Persistent fatigue that rest doesn't relieve.
- Feeling disconnected from your body or emotions.
- Difficulty accessing motivation or energy for activities you once enjoyed.
- Sense of being numb or going through the motions.
- Brain fog or difficulty concentrating.
- Feeling like you're watching your life from the outside.
- Depression or persistent low mood.

Signs of Nervous System Flexibility (Living in Your Window):

- The ability to feel activated when appropriate, then return to calm.
- Emotions that arise, peak, and naturally resolve.
- The capacity to stay present during difficult conversations or experiences.
- Physical tension releases naturally after stressful events.
- The ability to feel energized for challenges and relaxed during downtime.
- Resilience—bouncing back from setbacks without getting stuck.

Most people with emotional struggles are living primarily outside their window of tolerance, stuck in states that were once protective but have now become habitual and limiting.

The Revolutionary Science of Nervous System Regulation

Here's what changes everything: **your nervous system is not fixed.** Despite what you might have been told about your "anxious nature" or "tendency toward depression," your autonomic nervous system is remarkably responsive to intentional practices.

Research in polyvagal theory, developed by Dr. Stephen Porges, shows that we can learn to influence our nervous system states through specific techniques that work with the body's natural regulatory mechanisms. We can literally teach our nervous system new patterns, expanding our window of tolerance and developing what's called "nervous system flexibility."

This isn't about positive thinking or willpower—it's about working directly with the neurophysiological patterns that underlie emotional experience. When you learn to regulate your nervous system, you're not just managing symptoms—you're addressing the root cause of emotional dysregulation.

Rebecca's Journey: From Stuck to Flexible

When Rebecca first learned about nervous system states, she felt a profound sense of relief. "You mean this isn't just who I am? My body isn't permanently broken?" For years, she'd felt like her nervous system was her enemy, betraying her with its constant activation. Now she understood it was trying to protect her—it had just gotten stuck in an outdated pattern.

Rebecca began with simple practices to help her nervous system recognize safety. She started each morning by placing her hand on her heart and taking slow breaths, consciously signaling to her system that she was safe in that moment. Throughout the day, she practiced what's called "pendulation"—deliberately moving her attention between areas of activation and areas of calm in her body.

The breakthrough came in week three of her practice. Rebecca was in a stressful meeting when she felt her familiar activation beginning—heart racing, chest tightening, thoughts spinning. Instead of fighting the sensation or judging herself for it, she used a technique called "resourcing." She mentally recalled the feeling of her morning coffee ritual—the warmth of the mug in her hands, the peaceful quiet of her kitchen, and the sense of having that moment just for herself.

As she held both experiences—the stress of the meeting and the resourcefulness of her peaceful morning—something shifted. The activation didn't disappear, but it stopped escalating. She could feel her nervous system finding a middle ground, staying alert for the meeting while not spiraling into overwhelm.

"It was like teaching my body that it could handle stress without going into full panic mode," Rebecca explained. "I realized I didn't have to choose between being completely activated or completely shut down. There was a place in between."

The Four Pillars of Nervous System Regulation

Based on cutting-edge research in trauma therapy and neuroscience, I've identified four essential practices for developing nervous system flexibility:

1. Pendulation: Building Resilience Through Contrast

Pendulation involves deliberately moving your attention between areas of activation/discomfort and areas of calm/comfort. This practice teaches your nervous system that it can experience intensity without getting stuck there.

The Science: Pendulation works with your nervous system's natural tendency toward oscillation. Instead of staying frozen in one state, you're actively practicing moving between states, which builds flexibility and resilience.

The Practice: When you notice activation (anxiety, anger, overwhelm), instead of trying to eliminate it, find something in your current experience that feels neutral or pleasant. This might be:

- The feeling of your feet on the ground.
- A sense of support from your chair.
- The rhythm of your breathing.
- A pleasant memory or image.

Move your attention back and forth between the activation and the resource, spending 10–30 seconds on each. Notice how the activation may soften or change when contrasted with the resource.

2. Resourcing: Strengthening Your Body's Natural Calm

Resources are internal and external experiences that help your nervous system recognize safety and return to regulation. Building a robust collection of resources is like creating an internal pharmacy of calm.

Internal Resources include:

- Body-based resources: areas that feel comfortable, strong, or peaceful.
- Memory resources: times when you felt capable, loved, or successful.
- Imaginal resources: images, colors, or scenes that evoke calm.
- Relational resources: the felt sense of supportive relationships.

External Resources include:

- Nature: trees, water, sky, animals.
- Music or sounds that soothe your nervous system
- Scents that evoke safety or comfort.
- Physical objects that provide comfort or grounding.

The Practice: Spend time each day consciously connecting with your resources. Don't just think about them—feel them in your body. Notice how your breathing changes, how your muscles soften, and how your nervous system shifts when you truly connect with a resource.

3. Boundary Work: Using Your Body to Set Energetic Limits

Healthy boundaries are essential for nervous system regulation. When your boundaries are unclear or porous, your system stays activated, constantly trying to manage everyone else's energy and emotions.

Physical Boundary Practices:

- Notice your physical space and who or what is allowed into it.
- Practice sensing the edge of your body—where you end and the world begins.
- Use your arms to literally practice setting boundaries, pushing away imaginary intrusions.
- Work with your back—feeling supported, having something "behind" you.

Energetic Boundary Practices:

- Visualize a protective bubble or shield around your body.

- Practice "returning" other people's emotions instead of absorbing them.
- Notice when you're taking on responsibility that isn't yours and practice "giving it back."
- Use your breath to create a sense of your own energetic space.

4. Co-Regulation: Using Relationship and Environment for Support

Your nervous system doesn't regulate in isolation—it's designed to find balance through connection with other regulated systems. This includes both relationships with people and your relationship with your environment.

Relational Co-Regulation:

- Spend time with people whose presence helps you feel calm and centered.
- Practice being present with others without trying to fix or manage their emotional states.
- Learn to communicate your nervous system needs, for instance by saying, "I need a few minutes to settle before we talk about this."
- Develop relationships where emotional expression is safe and welcomed.

Environmental Co-Regulation:

- Spend time in nature, which naturally regulates human nervous systems.
- Create spaces in your home that calm your nervous system.
- Use lighting, sound, and scent to create regulatory environments.

- Notice which environments activate you and which help you feel settled.

Applying Regulation Skills to Rebecca's Daily Life

As Rebecca developed these nervous system regulation skills, her entire relationship with stress and emotion transformed. Instead of living in constant activation, she learned to surf the natural waves of nervous system arousal and recovery.

When work stress would spike her system into the fight/flight response, she'd use pendulation to move between the activation and a resource—often the memory of her garden, where she felt most peaceful. Instead of staying activated for hours, she could help her nervous system find regulation within minutes.

She developed a collection of reliable resources: the feeling of her dog's warm body against her leg, the sight of sunlight through her kitchen window, and the memory of her grandmother's hands teaching her to knead bread. These weren't just nice thoughts—they were neurophysiological tools that could shift her nervous system state.

Most importantly, Rebecca learned that regulation wasn't about never feeling stressed or activated. It was about developing the flexibility to move through different states without getting stuck. She could feel the intensity of a difficult day at work without carrying that activation home with her. She could experience the natural activation of excitement without it spiraling into anxiety.

The Window of Tolerance: Your Target Zone

The goal of nervous system regulation isn't to feel calm all the time—it's to expand your window of tolerance so you can experience the full range of human emotion without becoming dysregulated. In your optimal window, you can:

- Feel anger without losing control.
- Experience sadness without sinking into depression.
- Feel excitement without anxiety.
- Handle stress without chronic activation.
- Process difficult emotions without shutting down.
- Stay present in relationships even during conflict.
- Recover naturally from challenging experiences.

This is nervous system flexibility—the capacity to respond appropriately to life's demands while maintaining your essential sense of safety and connection.

Building Your Personal Regulation Tool Kit

Developing nervous system regulation is like physical fitness—it requires consistent practice, but the benefits compound over time. Each person's tool kit will be unique, based on their individual nervous system patterns, history, and preferences.

For Chronic Hyperactivation (stuck in fight/flight response), focus on:

- Practices that engage the parasympathetic nervous system (slow breathing, warm baths, gentle movement).
- Resources that emphasize safety and protection.
- Boundary work to reduce overstimulation.
- Environmental modifications to reduce triggers.

For Chronic Shutdown (stuck in freeze/collapse response), focus on:

- Gentle practices that bring energy and aliveness back into the system.

- Movement and breathwork that increase activation in small, manageable doses.
- Resources that connect you to vitality and joy.
- Social engagement to combat isolation.

For Nervous System Flexibility, maintain practices from both categories, learning to:

- Recognize your current state and what it needs.
- Move fluidly between activation and calm as situations require.
- Use co-regulation to support your individual regulation.
- Continually expand your window of tolerance.

Your Week 2 Action Plan: The Nervous System Regulation Implementation Guide

Building nervous system flexibility requires consistent, intentional practice. This week's action plan will guide you through developing the four core regulation skills while learning to recognize and expand your window of tolerance.

Day 1–2: Nervous System State Awareness

Morning State Check: Each morning, before getting out of bed, take two minutes to assess your nervous system state. Ask yourself:

- Do I feel activated (racing thoughts, tense muscles, restless energy)?
- Do I feel shut down (heavy, disconnected, unmotivated)?
- Do I feel in my window (calm but alert, present, capable)?

Rate your state on a simple scale: -3 (very shut down) to +3 (very activated), with 0 being your optimal window.

Hourly State Tracking: Set six reminders throughout your day. When the alarm sounds, quickly assess and rate your current nervous system state. Don't try to change anything—just notice patterns.

Evening State Review: Before sleeping, look at your day's ratings. What patterns do you notice? What times of day do you tend to be more activated or shut down? What activities or interactions seem to shift your state?

Key Goal: Develop awareness of your nervous system's natural rhythms and triggers.

Day 3–4: Pendulation Practice

Basic Pendulation Exercise: Find a mild area of tension or discomfort in your body. Rate its intensity 1–10. Now find an area that feels neutral or pleasant. Move your attention back and forth between these two areas, spending 15–30 seconds with each. After 2–3 minutes, re-rate the intensity of the uncomfortable area. Notice if it has shifted.

Emotional Pendulation: When you notice difficult emotions arising, practice pendulating between the emotion and a resource:

- Feel the emotion fully for 10–15 seconds.
- Shift attention to a resource (pleasant memory, body comfort, supportive relationship).
- Hold the resource for 10–15 seconds.
- Gently return to the emotion, noticing if it has changed.

- Continue pendulating until you feel some movement or shift.

Advanced Pendulation: Practice pendulating between current stress and resources during real-life situations. In meetings, conversations, or challenging moments, briefly connect with a resource while staying present to the situation.

Key Goal: Learn to move fluidly between activation and calm, building nervous system flexibility.

Day 5–6: Resource Building and Boundary Work

Resource Inventory: Create a comprehensive list:

- **Body Resources**: Areas that feel strong, comfortable, or peaceful.
- **Memory Resources**: Times you felt capable, loved, safe, or successful.
- **Imaginal Resources**: Images, colors, places, or scenarios that evoke calm.
- **Relational Resources**: People whose presence helps you feel regulated.
- **Environmental Resources**: Places, sounds, scents, or activities that support regulation.

Resource Strengthening: Choose 3–5 resources from your inventory. Spend five minutes each day consciously connecting with these resources. Don't just think about them—feel them in your body. Notice physical changes when you truly connect.

Physical Boundary Practice: Stand with your back against a wall. Feel the support behind you. Extend your arms out to your sides, defining your personal space. Practice saying "This is my space" while feeling the wall's support and your arms' protection.

Energetic Boundary Visualization: Imagine a protective bubble around your body. Experiment with different qualities: golden light, mirrors reflecting energy back, and a strong but permeable membrane. Find what feels most supportive for your nervous system.

Key Goal: Build a reliable tool kit of resources and establish clear energetic boundaries.

Day 7: Integration and Co-Regulation

Environmental Co-Regulation: Spend at least thirty minutes in a natural setting. Notice how your nervous system responds to trees, sky, water, or earth. Practice consciously receiving regulation from the natural world.

Relational Co-Regulation: Have a conversation with someone whose presence typically helps you feel calm. Instead of focusing on content, pay attention to how your nervous system responds to their energy, tone of voice, and presence.

Weekly Integration: Review your week's observations:

- What have you learned about your nervous system patterns?
- Which regulation techniques were most effective?
- What resources are most reliable for you?
- How has your window of tolerance shifted?

Personal Protocol Creation: Based on your week's experience, create your Nervous System First Aid Kit:

- Three go-to resources to use when you're activated.
- Three techniques to use when you're shut down.
- One daily practice for maintaining nervous system flexibility.

- One way to access co-regulation when you need support.

Weekly Success Metrics

By the end of Week 2, you should be able to:

- Recognize your nervous system state throughout the day.
- Successfully use pendulation to shift stuck states.
- Access at least five reliable resources that create a felt sense of calm.
- Implement basic boundary practices.
- Identify at least one form of co-regulation that supports your system.

Troubleshooting Common Challenges

"I can't feel the difference between states." This is common. Start with extreme examples—notice the difference between running upstairs (activation) and lying in bed (calm). Gradually work toward subtler distinctions.

"Pendulation makes me more activated." Go slower. Spend more time with the resource and less time with the activation. Make sure your resource truly feels calming in your body.

"I don't have any resources." Everyone has resources, though they may be small or forgotten. Start with basic ones: the feeling of ground under your feet, the sight of sky, or a single positive memory. Resources can be developed and strengthened over time.

"Nothing seems to regulate my nervous system." Some people need professional support, especially if trauma is involved. These practices should complement, not replace, appropriate therapeutic care.

Guided Nervous System Regulation Session: Finding Your Window of Tolerance

Allow approximately 20–25 minutes for this complete nervous system regulation experience.

Find a position that feels both comfortable and alert. You might sit with your back supported and feet on the ground or lie down with a pillow under your knees. The key is finding a position where your body feels held and supported while your mind can remain present and aware.

Take a moment to notice that by choosing to do this practice, you're prioritizing your nervous system's well-being. This is an act of self-care, a recognition that your nervous system regulation affects every aspect of your life—your emotions, relationships, health, and capacity for joy.

Begin by taking three natural breaths, not trying to change your breathing but simply noticing the rhythm that's already there. Your nervous system is constantly working to keep you alive and functioning, and your breath is one of its most important tools. With each breath, you're nourishing every cell in your body, supporting your system's natural capacity for healing and regulation.

Now, bring your attention to the places where your body makes contact with support. Feel the chair holding your body, the ground supporting your feet, and the earth beneath you providing stability. This is external co-regulation—your nervous system recognizing that you are held, supported, and not falling through space. Let yourself settle into this support, allowing your body to release any unnecessary effort or holding.

Let's begin by assessing your current nervous system state. Without trying to change anything, simply notice: Does your body feel activated? Perhaps you feel restless energy, tension, or a sense of being "revved up"? Or does your body feel shut down—heavy, tired, disconnected, or numb? Or perhaps you're somewhere in between—alert but calm, present but relaxed.

There's no right or wrong state to be in right now. Your nervous system is responding intelligently to your life circumstances, doing its best to keep you safe and functioning. We're simply developing the ability to recognize where you are and work skillfully with whatever state is present.

If you notice activation in your body—tension, restlessness, or agitation—let's practice finding something that feels more settled. This might be the feeling of your body being supported by the chair, the steady rhythm of your heartbeat, or simply the fact that in this moment, you are safe. You don't need to eliminate the activation—just find something that offers a different quality of experience.

Now, gently move your attention back and forth between the activation and this more settled feeling. Spend about ten seconds noticing the activated area, then ten seconds with the calmer area. This is pendulation—teaching your nervous system that it can experience intensity without getting stuck there, that it has options and flexibility.

If you're noticing shutdown or numbness, let's find a small spark of aliveness or energy. This might be the gentle rise and fall of your breath, a tiny movement in your fingers or toes, or even just the fact that you're here, present, choosing to tend to yourself. Again, you're not trying to force energy, just finding whatever vitality is available right now.

Pendulate between the shutdown area and this small source of life energy. Notice that even in shutdown, there's still life present—your heart beating, your lungs breathing, your system working to sustain you.

Now let's build your resource bank. Bring to mind a memory of a time when you felt genuinely calm and safe. This doesn't need to be a dramatic or significant event—perhaps a quiet moment in nature, a peaceful evening at home, or a time when you felt completely supported by someone you love.

Don't just think about this memory—really feel it in your body. Notice what happens to your breathing, your muscle tension, and your overall sense of well-being when you truly connect with this resource. Your nervous system doesn't distinguish between a real experience and a vividly remembered one—it responds to both as if they're happening now.

Spend a full minute soaking in this resource, letting it permeate your entire body. Notice how your nervous system shifts when it feels this quality of safety and calm. This is what regulation feels like—not necessarily the absence of all sensation, but a sense of being able to handle whatever arises.

Now, bring to mind another resource—perhaps a place in nature that makes you feel peaceful or an image that evokes a sense of protection and strength. Again, don't just visualize it—feel it in your body. Notice the physical shift that happens when you connect with this resource.

You're building what we call your "resource bank"—a collection of felt experiences that can help regulate your nervous system anytime you need support. These resources become more powerful the more you practice connecting with them.

Let's explore your physical boundaries. Imagine there's a protective bubble around your body. This boundary is permeable—it lets in what nourishes you and keeps out what drains or overwhelms you. Experiment with this boundary. Maybe it's made of golden light, or it's like a strong but flexible membrane, or it has mirrors on the outside that reflect others' energy back to them.

Feel how this boundary supports your nervous system's sense of safety. You have the right to your own energy, your own emotional space, and your own nervous system state. You don't have to absorb everyone else's anxiety, anger, or overwhelm.

Now, let's practice what's called "voo breathing"—a technique that directly activates your vagus nerve and supports nervous system regulation. Take a normal breath in, and as you exhale, make a low "voooo" sound, like the lowing of a cow. The vibration should be low and gentle, resonating in your chest and belly.

Try this three times, letting the vibration massage your internal organs and signal safety to your nervous system. This sound activates your parasympathetic nervous system—the part responsible for rest, digestion, and healing.

Let's end by setting an intention for nervous system flexibility. Imagine that instead of being stuck in one state—whether activation or shutdown—you have the flexibility to move fluidly through different states as life requires. You can feel excited without anxiety, sad without depression, and energized without overwhelm.

Visualize yourself moving through a typical day with this nervous system flexibility. You wake up feeling rested and alert. When challenges arise, you feel appropriately activated to handle them, then naturally return to calm afterward. When emotions arise, you feel them fully without being overwhelmed, letting them flow through you like weather patterns moving across the sky.

Take a moment to appreciate your nervous system—this incredible, complex network that works tirelessly to keep you alive, to help you respond to life's demands, and to connect you with others. Your nervous system isn't broken or defective—it's doing its best with the information and resources it has.

As you prepare to return to your day, remember that nervous system regulation is an ongoing practice, not a destination. There will be times when you feel activated or shut down, and that's normal. The goal isn't to feel calm all the time—it's to develop the flexibility to move through different states without getting stuck.

You now have tools: pendulation to build flexibility, resources to support regulation, boundaries to protect your energy, and the understanding that your nervous system is responsive to your intentional care. Each time you practice these skills, you're literally rewiring your nervous system, expanding your window of tolerance, and building resilience for whatever life brings.

When you're ready, take a deeper breath, gently move your fingers and toes, and slowly return your attention to the room around you. Notice if there's been any shift in your nervous system state. Carry this sense of regulation and these tools with you as you continue your day, knowing that you have the capacity to support your own nervous system's well-being.

Chapter 6

Week 3: Emotional Integration— Transforming Your Relationship with Feeling

When Emotions Become the Enemy

At 24, Jake thought he had life figured out. As a skilled electrician, he earned good money, had his own apartment, and could fix almost anything with his hands. But there was one thing he couldn't fix: the storm of emotions that seemed to hit him from nowhere. The crushing weight that would settle on his chest for weeks at a time, making even getting out of bed feel impossible. The anxiety that would spike when his boss criticized his work, leaving him shaking and unable to concentrate. The rage that would explode when his girlfriend asked about his drinking, leading to fights that left him feeling ashamed and more alone than ever.

Jake's solution was simple: numb it all. A few beers after work became a six-pack. Weekend drinking became weeknight drinking. When beer wasn't enough, he'd add pills—whatever he could find to quiet the emotional chaos in his chest. "I just want to feel normal," he'd tell himself as he cracked open another beer, already three deep and planning to keep going until the feelings stopped.

But the feelings never really stopped. They just went underground, building pressure like water behind a dam. The depression would break through anyway, hitting him with waves of hopelessness that made him question why he was alive. The anxiety would surge during hangovers, convincing him that everyone could see what a mess he was. The anger would erupt at random moments—at his coworkers, his girlfriend, drivers who cut him off—leaving destruction in its wake.

What Jake didn't understand was that he was at war with his own emotional intelligence. Every feeling he tried to numb was carrying vital information about his life, his needs, and his authentic self. His depression wasn't just random sadness—it was his system's way of saying he needed rest, connection, and time to grieve losses he'd never acknowledged. His anxiety wasn't weakness—it was his body's attempt to prepare him for challenges and alert him to situations where his boundaries were being violated. His anger wasn't just destructive rage—it was his authentic self fighting to be seen and respected.

By numbing these messengers, Jake was like a person unplugging fire alarms instead of addressing the fires they were warning about. The emotions kept coming because they had important work to do—work that couldn't be completed while he was chemically disconnected from his own experience.

The Revolutionary Approach: Emotions as Allies

Traditional approaches to emotional difficulties focus on managing, controlling, or eliminating problematic feelings. Depression is something to overcome. Anxiety is something to reduce. Anger is something to control. This adversarial relationship with emotions creates an internal war that's exhausting and ultimately futile.

This protocol offers a radically different approach: **learning to work with emotions as embodied messengers carrying important information about your needs, boundaries, and authentic self.** Instead of trying to silence these messengers, you'll learn to listen to them, understand their language, and work with the energy they provide.

This shift changes everything. Instead of being victimized by your emotions, you become curious about them. Instead of fighting feelings, you learn to dance with them. Instead of numbing emotional energy, you learn to transform it into fuel for positive change.

Understanding the Intelligence of Difficult Emotions

Each emotional state carries specific information and serves important functions when we learn to listen to its messages:

Depression's Hidden Intelligence: Depression often arises when your life has become disconnected from your authentic needs and values. Its heaviness may be your system's way of:

- Forcing you to slow down and rest when you've been pushing beyond your limits.
- Creating space to grieve losses you haven't acknowledged.
- Signaling that significant life changes are needed.

- Protecting you from overwhelming demands by reducing your energy output.
- Calling you to reconnect with what truly matters to you.

Anxiety's Protective Wisdom: Anxiety activates when your system perceives threats or challenges that require preparation or boundary-setting. Its activation may be:

- Alerting you to situations where your safety or well-being is at risk.
- Mobilizing energy to help you prepare for upcoming challenges.
- Signaling that your boundaries are being violated or tested.
- Highlighting discrepancies between your values and your actions.
- Preparing your system for necessary but difficult conversations or actions.

Anger's Authentic Voice: Anger arises when your values, boundaries, or authentic self are being violated or threatened. Its energy may be:

- Signaling that someone or something is crossing your boundaries.
- Mobilizing energy to protect what you care about.
- Alerting you to injustices that require your attention or action.
- Fighting for your right to be seen, heard, and respected.
- Providing fuel for necessary changes or difficult conversations.

Are You Fighting Your Own Emotional Intelligence?

As you consider Jake's story, reflect on your own relationship with difficult emotions. Perhaps you recognize patterns of:

Emotional Suppression

- Using substances, food, work, or other behaviors to avoid feeling.
- Telling yourself to "get over it" or "stop being so sensitive."
- Judging emotions as "bad," "weak," or "inappropriate."
- Pushing through emotional states without listening to their messages.
- Feeling ashamed of your emotional responses.

Emotional Overwhelm

- Getting swept away by emotional intensity.
- Feeling controlled by your emotions rather than informed by them.
- Experiencing emotions as endless or overwhelming.
- Unable to find the information or wisdom within emotional experiences.
- Feeling like emotions happen to you rather than communicate with you.

Emotional Numbing

- Feeling disconnected from your emotional experience.
- Using substances, behaviors, or dissociation to avoid feeling.
- Experiencing life as flat or colorless.
- Missing important information about your needs and boundaries.

- Making decisions without emotional input or wisdom.

If these patterns feel familiar, you're discovering that your relationship with emotions—not the emotions themselves—may be the source of much of your suffering.

Jake's Journey: From War to Alliance

When Jake first encountered the idea that his emotions might be allies rather than enemies, he was skeptical. "My depression makes me useless. My anxiety ruins everything. My anger destroys my relationships. How can these be helpful?" But he was tired of the cycle—drinking to numb, feeling worse, drinking more—and desperate enough to try a different approach.

Jake started with what seemed like the simplest step: instead of immediately reaching for a beer when emotions arose, he would spend five minutes just feeling them in his body. The first time he tried this with depression, he was shocked by what he discovered.

Sitting with the heavy feeling in his chest instead of drinking it away, Jake began to notice layers within the depression. Underneath the familiar weight was grief—grief for his father, who had died two years earlier and whose death Jake had never properly mourned. There was also exhaustion—not just physical tiredness, but soul-deep fatigue from trying to be someone he wasn't, working a job that felt meaningless, and living a life that didn't reflect his values.

"I realized my depression wasn't random," Jake explained later. "It was trying to tell me I needed to slow down, to cry for my dad, to figure out what actually mattered to me. When I kept drinking it away, it had to keep getting louder and stronger to get through to me."

With anxiety, Jake discovered it often arose when his boundaries were being crossed—when his boss dumped extra work on him without asking, when his girlfriend tried to control his behavior, and when friends pressured him to drink more than he wanted. The anxiety wasn't weakness—it was his system trying to alert him to these boundary violations so he could respond appropriately.

Most surprising was what he found within his anger. Underneath the explosive rage was his authentic self fighting for respect, recognition, and the right to be seen. His anger emerged when people dismissed his ideas, when he felt invisible or unheard, and when his values were trampled. The anger wasn't the problem—the problem was that he'd never learned to express his authentic needs and boundaries before they built up into explosive rage.

Jake learned to work with his emotions rather than against them. When depression arose, instead of drinking, he would ask: "What do I need right now? What am I grieving? What changes need to happen in my life?" When anxiety spiked, he'd investigate. "What boundary is being crossed? What do I need to prepare for? How can I create more safety?" When anger emerged, he'd explore. "What values are being violated? What do I need to say or do? How can I express this energy constructively?"

The Four Pillars of Emotional Integration

Based on research in emotion regulation, somatic therapy, and neuroscience, emotional integration involves four essential skills:

1. Emotional Mapping: Learning Your Body's Unique Language

Every person experiences emotions differently in their body. Depression might feel like heaviness in your chest or emptiness in your belly. Anxiety might manifest as tension in your shoulders or fluttering in your stomach. Anger might appear as heat in your face or clenching in your jaw. Learning your unique emotional map is essential for working skillfully with feelings.

The Practice: Throughout the day, when you notice emotions arising, pause and scan your body and ask:

- Where do I feel this emotion most strongly?
- What does it feel like (heavy, tight, hot, cold, moving, stuck)?
- How big is it? What's its texture or quality?
- Is it changing as I pay attention to it?

Create a personal emotion map, noting how different feelings show up in your unique body. This map becomes your early warning system and your guide for working with emotional energy.

Why It Works: When you can identify the physical signature of emotions, you can work with them at the body level rather than just mentally. This creates more options for response and regulation.

2. Message Translation: Understanding What Emotions Are Communicating

Once you can feel emotions in your body, the next step is learning to decode their messages. Each emotion carries information about your needs, boundaries, values, and authentic self.

The Practice: When you feel an emotion arising, instead of trying to change it, get curious about its message:

For Depression, ask:

- What do I need to rest from or slow down?
- What losses do I need to grieve?
- What parts of my life no longer serve me?
- What values or dreams have I abandoned?
- What would bring genuine meaning to my life?

For Anxiety, ask:

- What do I need to prepare for or pay attention to?
- Where are my boundaries being violated?
- What situations feel unsafe and why?
- What do I need to feel more secure?
- What actions would help me feel more prepared?

For Anger, ask:

- What values of mine are being violated?
- What boundaries need to be set or defended?
- What do I need to say or do to honor my authentic self?
- How can I use this energy constructively?
- What injustice needs my attention or action?

Why It Works: When you understand emotions as information rather than problems, you can use their intelligence to make better decisions and create more authentic lives.

3. Integration Techniques: Working with Stuck Emotional Patterns

Sometimes emotions get stuck in the body, creating chronic patterns of depression, anxiety, or anger. Integration techniques help you work with these stuck patterns somatically, allowing emotional energy to flow and complete naturally.

Breathing with Emotions: When you feel stuck in emotional energy, breathe directly into the area where you feel it. Don't try to breathe it away—breathe with it, giving it space and oxygen.

Movement and Expression: Allow the emotion to have appropriate expression through movement. Depression might want slow, heavy movements or curling up. Anxiety might need shaking, walking, or stretching. Anger might want pushing movements or vocal expression.

Dialogue with Emotions: Literally speak with your emotions. Ask what they need, what they're trying to tell you, and how you can work together. You might be surprised by the wisdom that emerges.

Pendulation with Emotions: Move your attention between the emotional sensation and a resource (peaceful memory, body comfort, supportive relationship). This teaches your system that it can feel emotions without being overwhelmed by them.

Why It Works: These techniques work with emotions at the somatic level, allowing stuck energy to move and complete rather than remaining trapped in the body.

4. Alchemy Practices: Transforming Emotional Energy

The goal isn't to eliminate difficult emotions but to transform their energy into fuel for positive change. Every emotion carries power that can be channeled constructively.

Depression's Energy for Deep Change: The inward focus and reduced activity of depression can be channeled into:

- Deep reflection about what truly matters to you.
- Grieving processes that free up energy for new growth.
- Rest and restoration that your system genuinely needs.

- Identifying and releasing what no longer serves you.

Anxiety's Energy for Preparation and Protection: The activated energy of anxiety can be transformed into:

- Thorough preparation for challenges.
- Setting and maintaining healthy boundaries.
- Taking protective action where needed.
- Channeling worry into productive planning.

Anger's Energy for Authentic Action: The mobilized force of anger can become:

- Energy for setting and defending boundaries.
- Fuel for standing up for your values.
- Power for making necessary changes.
- Motivation for fighting injustice or protecting others.

The Practice: When you feel difficult emotions, instead of trying to eliminate them, ask, "How can I use this energy constructively? What positive action does this emotion want to fuel? How can I channel this power toward what matters to me?"

Applying Emotional Integration to Jake's Transformation

As Jake developed these emotional integration skills, his entire relationship with feelings transformed. Instead of seeing emotions as enemies to be numbed, he began experiencing them as allies carrying important information about his life.

When depression arose, Jake learned to ask what it was trying to tell him. Often, it was signaling that he needed rest, time to grieve his father, or changes in his work life. Instead of drinking the depression away, he would honor its messages—taking time off when possible, visiting his father's grave, and exploring different career possibilities.

His anxiety became an early warning system for boundary violations. When it spiked at work, Jake learned to check whether he was being asked to do more than he could handle or work in unsafe conditions. The anxiety's message helped him have conversations with his boss about workload and safety protocols that ultimately improved his job satisfaction.

Most dramatically, Jake's relationship with anger transformed. Instead of letting it build to explosive levels, he learned to listen to its messages about respect and authenticity. When anger arose, he'd ask what boundary needed protection or what value was being violated. This allowed him to address issues before they became relationship-ending explosions.

Jake's drinking decreased naturally as he developed these skills. He still enjoyed a beer after work sometimes, but it wasn't about numbing—it was about genuine enjoyment. "When I stopped fighting my emotions and started listening to them," Jake reflected, "I didn't need to drink them away anymore. They became my guides instead of my enemies."

The Wisdom Hidden in Your Difficult Emotions

Perhaps the most radical shift in emotional integration is recognizing that your most difficult emotions often carry your deepest wisdom. The depression that feels so heavy might be your soul's way of calling you toward a more authentic life. The anxiety that feels so overwhelming might be your system's attempt to protect what you care about most. The anger that feels so destructive might be your authentic self fighting for recognition and respect.

This doesn't mean all emotions should be acted on directly—part of emotional intelligence is learning when to feel without immediately acting. But it does mean that every emotion deserves to be heard, understood, and respected for the information it carries.

When you stop fighting your emotions and start working with them, you discover that they're not your enemies—they're your allies in creating a life that truly reflects who you are and what you value.

Building Your Emotional Integration Practice

Developing emotional integration skills requires patience, curiosity, and self-compassion. You're not trying to become someone who never feels difficult emotions—you're learning to work skillfully with the full spectrum of human feelings.

Daily Emotional Check-ins: Several times each day, pause and ask, "What am I feeling right now? Where do I feel it in my body? What might it be trying to tell me?"

Weekly Emotional Review: Once a week, reflect on the emotions you've experienced and what messages they might have been carrying. Look for patterns and themes.

Monthly Life Assessment: Use your emotional feedback to assess whether your life is aligned with your authentic needs and values. What changes might your emotions be calling for?

Substance Use Awareness: If you use substances to manage emotions, begin noticing what feelings you're trying to avoid and what messages they might carry. Consider reducing numbing behaviors gradually as you develop integration skills.

Your Week 3 Action Plan: The Emotional Integration Implementation Guide

This week focuses on transforming your relationship with emotions from adversarial to collaborative. You'll learn to map your unique emotional landscape, decode the messages your feelings carry, and begin using emotional energy as fuel for positive change.

Day 1–2: Personal Emotional Mapping

Morning Emotion Inventory: Each morning, spend five minutes doing a complete emotional body scan. Notice:

- What emotions are present as you wake up?
- Where do you feel them in your body?
- What physical sensations accompany each emotion?
- How intense are they on a scale of 1–10?

Emotional Mapping Exercise: Create three columns in your journal with the headings Emotion, Body Location, and Physical Description. Throughout these two days, every time you notice an emotion, record:

- The specific emotion (sad, worried, frustrated, excited, etc.).
- Where you feel it most strongly in your body.
- How it feels physically (tight, heavy, warm, buzzing, etc.).

Evening Pattern Recognition: Before sleep, review your emotional map. What patterns do you notice? Do certain emotions always show up in the same body locations? Do they have consistent physical qualities?

Key Goal: Develop awareness of your unique emotional-physical signature patterns.

Day 3–4: Message Translation Practice

Real-Time Message Decoding: When emotions arise, instead of trying to change them, pause and ask the relevant questions:

For any depressive feelings:

- What do I need to slow down or rest from?
- What losses might I need to grieve?
- What parts of my life no longer serve my authentic self?
- What would bring genuine meaning to my current situation?

For anxious feelings:

- What might I need to prepare for or pay attention to?
- Where might my boundaries be violated?
- What would help me feel safer in this situation?
- What action would help me feel more prepared?

For angry feelings:

- What values of mine might be being disrespected?
- What boundaries need to be set or defended?
- What does my authentic self need to express?
- How can I use this energy constructively?

Message Journaling: Record not just the emotions you feel, but the messages you discover within them. Look for themes and patterns in what your emotions are trying to tell you.

Key Goal: Learn to decode the wisdom and information within difficult emotions.

Day 5–6: Integration Techniques and Somatic Work

Breathing with Emotions Exercise: When you feel stuck with emotional energy:

1. Locate where you feel the emotion in your body.
2. Place your hand on that area if comfortable.
3. Breathe directly into that space for 2–3 minutes.
4. Don't try to breathe the emotion away—breathe with it, giving it space.

Emotional Movement Practice: Allow emotions to express themselves through movement:

- Depression: Try slow, grounding movements or curling up in a supportive way.
- Anxiety: Experiment with shaking, walking, or stretching.
- Anger: Try pushing movements against a wall or vigorous walking.

Dialogue with Emotions: Spend ten minutes each day literally talking with a difficult emotion and ask:

- "Depression, what do you need me to know?"
- "Anxiety, what are you trying to protect me from?"
- "Anger, what values of mine are you defending?"

Write down what emerges from these conversations.

Key Goal: Develop somatic skills for working with stuck emotional patterns.

Day 7: Emotional Alchemy and Integration

Energy Transformation Practice: Choose one difficult emotion you've worked with this week and ask:

- How can I use this emotion's energy constructively?
- What positive action does this feeling want to fuel?
- How can I channel this power toward what matters to me?

Weekly Emotional Wisdom Review: Look back through your week's emotional experiences and ask:

- What have my emotions been trying to teach me?
- What patterns do I notice in my emotional messages?
- What changes might my emotions be calling for in my life?
- How has my relationship with difficult feelings shifted?

Life Alignment Assessment: Use your emotional feedback to assess your current life and ask yourself:

- What aspects of my life consistently generate negative emotions?
- What activities, relationships, or situations consistently generate positive emotions?
- What changes would better align my life with my authentic needs and values?

Integration Planning: Based on the week's discoveries, identify:

- Three key messages your emotions have been sending.
- Two life changes your emotional wisdom is calling for.
- One way you can use emotional energy more constructively.

Weekly Success Metrics

By the end of Week 3, you should be able to:

- Identify the physical location and sensation of at least five different emotions.
- Successfully decode the message within at least one difficult emotion.
- Use at least one somatic technique to work with stuck emotional energy.
- Channel emotional energy toward constructive action at least once.
- Notice a shift in your relationship with difficult emotions.

Troubleshooting Common Challenges

"I can't feel any emotions." This often indicates emotional numbing as a protective mechanism. Start with physical sensations (tired, tense, restless) and work gradually toward emotional awareness. Consider whether substances or behaviors might be interfering with feeling.

"My emotions feel too overwhelming." Go slower. Start with less intense emotions. Use pendulation between the emotion and a resource. If emotions feel unmanageable, consider professional support.

"I don't trust my emotions." This is common, especially if you've been taught emotions are dangerous or unreliable. Start with curiosity rather than trust. You don't have to act on every emotional message—just listen to them.

"My emotions tell me to do destructive things." Learning to decode emotional messages is different from acting on emotional impulses. The message within anger might be "set a boundary," but the action might be a calm conversation, not yelling. Always filter emotional messages through your values and wisdom.

Guided Emotional Integration Session: Dancing with Feeling

Allow approximately 25–30 minutes for this complete emotional integration experience.

Find a comfortable position where you feel both supported and free to move if needed. This practice may bring up emotions, so ensure you're in a space where you feel safe to feel whatever arises. Remember that emotions are temporary visitors—they arise, peak, and naturally pass when we don't resist or amplify them.

Take a moment to set an intention for this practice. Perhaps it's to develop a more collaborative relationship with your emotions, to understand what they're trying to tell you, or simply to practice being present with whatever you're feeling without needing to change it immediately.

Begin with several natural breaths, noticing that your breath continues without any effort from you. Your body knows how to breathe, just as it knows how to feel. Emotions are as natural as breathing—they're part of your body's intelligence system, providing constant information about your experience and your needs.

Let's start by scanning your current emotional landscape. Without trying to change anything, simply notice: What emotions are present right now? You might notice anxiety about doing this practice, curiosity about what you'll discover, sadness that's been lingering, or perhaps a mix of feelings. There's no right or wrong emotional state for this practice.

Now, let's create a foundation of safety and resources before we explore more difficult emotions. Bring to mind something or someone that makes you feel genuinely cared for and supported. This might be a person who loves you, a pet, a place in nature, or even a part of yourself that's wise and compassionate.

Don't just think about this resource—really feel it in your body. Notice how your breathing changes, how your muscles soften, and how your nervous system shifts when you connect with this sense of being cared for. This resource will be available to you throughout this practice if you need to return to safety.

Now, gently bring to awareness an emotion that's been challenging for you recently. This doesn't need to be your most difficult emotion—choose something manageable that you're willing to explore. Maybe it's frustration about work, sadness about a relationship, or anxiety about the future.

Instead of trying to solve or eliminate this emotion, simply notice where you feel it in your body. Is it in your chest, your stomach, your shoulders, or your throat? How big is it? What does it feel like? Heavy, tight, buzzing, burning, or cold? Just observe with curiosity, as if you're a scientist studying an interesting phenomenon.

Now, instead of judging this emotion as good or bad, let's get curious about what it might be trying to communicate. If this emotion could speak to you, what would it say? What might it be trying to protect you from or guide you toward?

If you're feeling sadness, perhaps it's honoring a loss, calling you to slow down, or highlighting something that matters deeply to you. If you're experiencing anxiety, maybe it's trying to prepare you for something important, alerting you to a boundary that needs attention, or mobilizing energy for necessary action. If anger is present, it might be defending your values, fighting for your authentic self, or signaling that respect is needed.

Listen to your emotion without immediately acting on what it says. You're not committing to anything—you're simply receiving information from your body's wisdom. What does this emotion know that your thinking mind might have missed?

Now, notice the energy within this emotion. Emotions aren't just feelings—they're also energy that can be channeled and transformed. Depression carries the energy of depth and reflection. Anxiety holds the power of preparation and protection. Anger contains the force of boundaries and authentic action.

Ask your emotion, "How can I use your energy wisely? What positive action do you want to fuel? How can your power serve my highest good?" Don't force an answer—simply listen with curiosity.

You might discover that your sadness wants to fuel deeper connections with people you care about. Your anxiety might want to channel its energy into thorough preparation for an upcoming challenge. Your anger might want to power a difficult but necessary conversation about respect and boundaries.

Let's practice what's called "pendulation" with your emotion. Focus on the emotional sensation for about ten seconds, really feeling it in your body. Then shift your attention to your resource—that sense of being cared for and supported—for about ten seconds. Move back and forth between the emotion and the resource several times.

Notice what happens as you pendulate. Often, the emotion can soften, shift, or reveal new layers when it's held alongside safety and support. You're teaching your nervous system that it can feel emotions without being overwhelmed by them.

Now, if your emotion has been stuck or repetitive, let's try giving it some movement. Emotions are energy that want to flow, but sometimes they get trapped in our bodies. If it feels right for you, allow your emotion to express itself through gentle movement.

If you're working with sadness, you might curl up in a supportive way or make slow, flowing movements. If anxiety is present, you might try gentle shaking, stretching, or walking in place. If anger is there, you might push against the wall or make strong, contained movements.

Let the emotion move through you rather than staying stuck. Remember, the goal isn't to eliminate the emotion but to allow it to flow and complete naturally.

Take a moment to thank your emotion for the information it's provided. Even if it's been difficult or uncomfortable, it's been trying to serve you, to protect you, and to guide you toward something important. Your emotions are part of your body's intelligence system—they deserve respect and appreciation, not rejection or suppression.

Now, let's expand your awareness to include your whole emotional ecosystem. Notice that emotions are like weather patterns—they arise, intensify, and naturally pass when we don't resist them. You are not your emotions—you are the sky in which emotions move like clouds.

Set an intention for how you want to work with your emotions going forward. Perhaps it's to listen more carefully to their messages, to stop fighting them so intensely, or to use their energy more constructively. What would it be like to have your emotions as allies rather than enemies?

Imagine yourself moving through your daily life with this new relationship to emotions. When depression arises, instead of fighting it, you get curious about what it's trying to tell you about rest, grieving, or life changes. When anxiety spikes, instead of trying to eliminate it, you ask what it's trying to prepare you for or protect you from. When anger emerges, instead of suppressing it, you listen to what values it's defending or what boundaries it's calling for.

Visualize yourself using emotional energy constructively—channeling anxiety into thorough preparation, transforming anger into boundary-setting conversations using depression's inward focus for deep reflection about what truly matters to you.

As you prepare to complete this practice, take a moment to appreciate your courage. It takes bravery to feel emotions fully in a culture that often encourages numbing and suppression. By learning to work with your emotions rather than against them, you're developing emotional intelligence and resilience.

Remember that this is an ongoing practice. There will be times when emotions feel overwhelming, and that's normal. The goal isn't to never struggle with feelings—it's to develop the skills to work with them more skillfully, to hear their messages, and to use their energy in service of your authentic life.

Your emotions are not your enemies—they're your allies in creating a life that truly reflects who you are and what you value. Each feeling carries information about your needs, your boundaries, your values, and your path forward. When you learn to listen to this information and work with emotional energy constructively, you become the author of your own emotional experience rather than its victim.

When you're ready, take a deeper breath, move your body gently, and slowly return your attention to the space around you. Carry this sense of emotional wisdom and integration with you, knowing that you have the tools to work collaboratively with whatever feelings arise in your life.

Chapter 7

Week 4: Somatic Cognitive Integration— Bridging Body and Mind

When Your Body Remembers What Your Mind Tries to Forget

At 35, Maria had built what looked like a successful life. She had a master's degree in social work, helped other trauma survivors for a living, and maintained an apartment filled with books on healing and self-development. But inside her mind, a relentless voice ran a constant loop of criticism and catastrophe: *"You're not good enough. Something terrible is about to happen. You can't trust anyone. You're damaged goods."*

These thoughts weren't just mental noise—they lived in her body with physical precision. When the familiar thought *"I'm going to mess this up"* arose before work presentations, her chest would constrict, her breathing would become shallow, and her hands would shake. When the voice whispered, *"People will leave you if they really know you,"* her stomach would clench, her shoulders would hunch forward protectively, and she'd feel herself literally shrinking inward.

Maria knew where these patterns came from. Growing up with an alcoholic father and depressed mother, she'd learned early that survival meant predicting danger, staying small, and never expecting safety. By age eight, she was hypervigilant, scanning her parents' faces for signs of the next explosion or shutdown. By twelve, she'd internalized the message that she was responsible for everyone else's emotions and that her own needs were burdens.

Now, decades later, Maria understood intellectually that these childhood messages were no longer accurate. She could explain trauma responses to her clients with expertise and compassion. But when triggered, her body would respond as if she were still that frightened child, and her mind would flood with the same survival thoughts that had once kept her safe but now kept her trapped.

"I know better," she would tell herself after another panic attack triggered by her supervisor's neutral tone. "I know these thoughts aren't rational. I know I'm safe now." But knowing hadn't been enough to stop the patterns. Her attempts at cognitive restructuring—challenging negative thoughts, practicing positive affirmations, and analyzing her thinking errors—provided temporary relief but never touched the deeper integration where thoughts and physical states were locked together in trauma-informed loops.

What Maria didn't yet understand was that her thoughts and body sensations weren't separate systems influencing each other—they were one integrated network that had been shaped by her early experiences and needed to be healed as a unified whole.

The Illusion of Separate Systems

Traditional approaches to emotional healing often treat thoughts and physical sensations as separate systems. Cognitive therapies focus on changing thinking patterns, assuming the body will follow. Somatic therapies work with physical sensations, hoping mental patterns will shift. While both approaches offer valuable tools, they miss a fundamental reality: **thoughts and physical states are inseparable aspects of one integrated system.**

Every thought has a physical component. When you think, *I'm in danger,* your nervous system immediately responds with increased heart rate, muscle tension, and stress hormones. When you think, *I'm loved and safe,* your body releases different chemicals, your muscles soften, and your breathing deepens.

Conversely, every physical state influences your thinking. When your body is tense and activated, your mind naturally scans for threats and problems. When your body is relaxed and open, your thoughts tend toward optimism and possibility.

This integration is especially profound for people who've experienced trauma or adverse childhood experiences (ACEs). Traumatic experiences create what researchers call "embodied cognitions"—thought patterns that are literally held in the body's tissues, nervous system, and cellular memory. These patterns can't be changed through thinking alone because they exist at the intersection of mind and body.

Understanding Trauma's Mind-Body Signature

Adverse childhood experiences create specific patterns of somatic cognitive integration that can persist well into adulthood:

Hypervigilance Patterns: The body maintains chronic tension and alertness while the mind constantly scans for danger, criticism, or rejection. Thoughts like *What's wrong here? What should I be worried about?* are paired with physical states of activation and readiness.

Collapse Patterns: The body moves into shutdown and fatigue while the mind generates thoughts of hopelessness, worthlessness, or futility. Physical depletion reinforces thoughts like *Nothing I do matters. I'm too broken to heal.*

Freeze Patterns: The body becomes immobilized while the mind dissociates or goes blank. Physical numbness supports thoughts like *I'm not really here. This isn't happening to me.*

Fawn Patterns: The body takes on appeasing postures while the mind focuses obsessively on others' needs and reactions. Physical contraction pairs with thoughts like *What do they need from me? How can I make them comfortable?*

These patterns made perfect sense in childhood—they were intelligent adaptations to impossible circumstances. But when they persist into adulthood, they create suffering because the integrated mind-body system continues responding to current situations as if they were past traumas.

Are You Carrying Childhood Patterns in Your Adult Body?

As you consider Maria's experience, reflect on your own somatic cognitive patterns. Perhaps you recognize:

Anxiety Patterns

- Physical tension paired with catastrophic thinking
- Racing heart combined with "what if" mental loops.
- Shallow breathing alongside scanning for problems or threats.
- Muscle tightness linked to thoughts about future disasters.

Depression Patterns

- Heavy, collapsed body posture combined with self-critical thoughts.
- Fatigue and low energy paired with hopeless or worthless thinking.
- Slumped shoulders linked to thoughts like "I'm a burden" or "Nothing matters."
- Physical withdrawal matching mental isolation and disconnection.

Anger Patterns

- Clenched muscles paired with thoughts about unfairness or disrespect.
- Heat and tension combined with mental rehearsal of confrontations.
- Rigid posture linked to thoughts about being misunderstood or violated.
- Physical mobilization matching mental preparation for battle.

Trauma Response Patterns

- Body bracing combined with thoughts about imminent danger.

- Physical numbness paired with dissociative or "checking out" thoughts.
- Hypervigilant body scanning linked to constant mental threat assessment.
- Collapsed or small physical posture combined with thoughts about being powerless.

If these patterns feel familiar, you're discovering how your early experiences created integrated mind-body responses that continue to shape your adult life.

Maria's Journey: Healing the Split Between Knowing and Feeling

When Maria first learned about somatic cognitive integration, she felt both relief and frustration. Relief because it explained why positive thinking and cognitive restructuring hadn't been enough. Frustration because it meant her healing journey was going to be more complex than just changing her thoughts.

Maria began with simple practices to track how her thoughts showed up in her body. She discovered that her most problematic thoughts had very specific physical signatures. The thought *I'm not safe* always appeared with tension in her upper back and shoulders hunching forward. The thought *I'm too much for people* came with a collapse in her chest and a pulling inward of her arms.

More importantly, she noticed that these physical patterns often preceded the thoughts. Her body would begin to contract and brace before her mind consciously registered danger. Her nervous system was responding to cues from her environment—a certain tone of voice, a facial expression, an interpersonal dynamic—that reminded her unconsciously of childhood experiences.

The breakthrough came when Maria learned to work with both dimensions simultaneously. Instead of trying to think her way out of trauma responses, she began using somatic cognitive restructuring. When she noticed her body beginning to contract with the familiar "I'm not safe" pattern, instead of fighting the thought, she would:

1. **Acknowledge the body pattern**: "I notice my shoulders hunching and my chest tightening."

2. **Recognize the thought pattern**: "The story 'I'm not safe' is arising."

3. **Provide somatic resources**: Consciously soften her shoulders, breathe into her chest, and feel her feet on the ground.

4. **Offer updated information**: "I notice this pattern from childhood. Right now, in this moment, I can create safety by breathing and grounding."

"It wasn't about convincing myself I was safe," Maria explained later. "It was about giving my nervous system different information through my body while acknowledging the old pattern with compassion. My body had to feel the safety, not just my mind."

The integration worked both ways. As Maria's body learned to relax and open, her thoughts naturally became more flexible and optimistic. As she developed cognitive awareness of her trauma patterns, she could use that awareness to guide somatic interventions before the patterns became overwhelming.

The Four Foundations of Somatic Cognitive Integration

Based on research in trauma therapy, neuroscience, and embodied cognition, somatic cognitive integration involves four essential skills:

1. Thought-Body Tracking: Recognizing Integrated Patterns

The first step in integration is developing an awareness of how thoughts and physical sensations work together in your unique system. Every person has different patterns of how mental and physical states interweave.

The Practice: Throughout the day, when you notice strong thoughts or emotions, pause and track both dimensions:

Mental Tracking: What specific thoughts are present?

- Are they past-focused, future-focused, or present-focused?
- Are they self-critical, other-critical, or threat-focused?
- Do they involve "should" statements, catastrophizing, or all-or-nothing thinking?
- What stories are they telling about yourself, others, or the world?

Physical Tracking: How do these thoughts show up in your body?

- Where do you feel tension, contraction, or activation?
- What's happening with your breathing, posture, and muscle tone?
- Are you bracing, collapsing, or mobilizing?
- What's the overall felt sense in your body?

Integration Mapping: Create a personal map of your thought-body patterns. You might discover that perfectionist thoughts always come with jaw clenching or that abandonment fears always pair with chest constriction.

Why It Works: Awareness of integrated patterns gives you multiple points of intervention. You can work with the thought, the physical state, or the connection between them.

2. Somatic Cognitive Restructuring: Using the Body to Support Mental Flexibility

Traditional cognitive restructuring tries to change thoughts through logic and evidence. Somatic cognitive restructuring uses body-based interventions to create the physical foundation for new thinking patterns.

The Process:

1. **Notice the integrated pattern**: "I'm having the thought *I'm going to fail*, and my chest is tightening."

2. **Provide somatic support**: Breathe into your chest, soften your shoulders, and feel your feet on the ground.

3. **Create physical resources**: Find areas of your body that feel strong, comfortable, or neutral.

4. **Offer updated information from this resourced state**: "I notice this old pattern. From this more grounded place, I can see other possibilities."

Key Principle: Don't try to argue with trauma-based thoughts while your body is in a trauma state. First provide somatic resources, then engage with cognitive flexibility.

Why It Works: When your nervous system feels safe and grounded, your thinking naturally becomes more flexible and realistic. You're not forcing positive thoughts—you're creating the conditions where more balanced thinking can emerge.

3. Integration Exercises: Working with Mind and Body as One System

These practices work directly with the connection between thoughts and sensations, treating them as one unified experience rather than separate systems.

Breathing with Thoughts: When distressing thoughts arise, instead of trying to change them, breathe directly into the physical sensation they create. Often, when the physical component shifts, the thought naturally transforms.

Embodied Affirmations: Instead of just repeating positive statements, create affirmations that include both mental and physical components: "I am safe" (while feeling your feet on the ground), "I am worthy" (while opening your chest and lengthening your spine).

Thought-Body Dialogue: Have conversations between your thinking mind and your body wisdom. Ask your body what it needs when certain thoughts arise. Ask your mind what story it's trying to protect you with when your body contracts.

Pendulation Between States: Move back and forth between the thought-body pattern that's stuck and a more resourced thought-body state. This teaches your system flexibility and choice.

Why It Works: These exercises train your nervous system to experience mind and body as integrated rather than in conflict, creating more options for response.

4. Pattern Interruption: Using Physical Shifts to Change Mental Loops

Sometimes trauma-based thought patterns become so automatic they feel unstoppable. Physical pattern interruption can break these loops before they gain momentum.

Movement Interruption: When you notice familiar thought loops beginning, engage in physical movement that's incompatible with the pattern. If anxiety thoughts come with a forward head posture, deliberately lengthen your spine. If depressive thoughts come with a collapsed chest, open your arms wide.

Posture Shifting: Consciously change your physical posture when you notice problematic thought patterns. Stand tall when self-critical thoughts arise. Open your arms when thoughts of isolation emerge.

Sensory Interruption: Use your senses to interrupt mental loops. Feel different textures, listen to specific sounds, and look at colors or patterns that help ground you in present-moment experience.

Breath Pattern Changes: Shift your breathing pattern to interrupt thought loops. Use longer exhales to calm anxiety-based thinking or energizing breathing to lift depressive thought patterns.

Why It Works: Since thoughts and physical states are integrated, changing one automatically influences the other. Physical interruption can stop mental loops before they become overwhelming.

Applying Integration to Maria's Daily Life

As Maria developed these somatic cognitive integration skills, her relationship with her trauma responses transformed completely. Instead of being at the mercy of automatic patterns, she developed the ability to work skillfully with the intersection of mind and body.

When her familiar "I'm not good enough" thought arose before presentations, Maria would notice its physical signature—the hunched shoulders and tight chest—and provide somatic support before engaging cognitively. She'd breathe into her chest, lengthen her spine, and feel her feet on the ground. From this more resourced physical state, she could acknowledge the old pattern with compassion. "I notice this familiar protection from childhood. Right now, I have skills and knowledge to share that can help people."

Her hypervigilance patterns began to shift as she learned to interrupt the thought-body loops before they gained momentum. When she noticed her body beginning to scan for danger and her mind starting to catastrophize, she'd consciously soften her gaze, relax her jaw, and redirect her attention to present-moment sensory information.

Most significantly, Maria learned to distinguish between her adult self and her childhood trauma responses. "I realized that the scared, vigilant part of me was still trying to protect the child I once was," she reflected. "When I could acknowledge that protection with gratitude while also giving my adult body and mind different information, everything started to shift."

The Neuroplasticity of Integrated Healing

Perhaps the most hopeful aspect of somatic cognitive integration is its relationship to neuroplasticity—your brain's ability to form new neural pathways throughout your life. When you practice working with thoughts and physical states as one integrated system, you're literally rewiring the neural networks that were shaped by early experiences.

Traditional approaches that work with thoughts or body sensations separately create some new neural pathways, but integrated approaches create more comprehensive rewiring. You're not just learning new thoughts or new body patterns—you're learning new ways of being that encompass your whole system.

This is especially important for trauma healing. Trauma creates integrated patterns of mind-body response, and healing happens most effectively when it addresses the same integrated system. You're not trying to override your trauma responses—you're creating new, more flexible patterns that can coexist with and gradually replace the old ones.

Building Your Somatic Cognitive Integration Practice

Developing integration skills requires patience and self-compassion, especially if you're working with trauma-based patterns. Remember that these patterns developed as intelligent protection, and they deserve gratitude even as you're creating new options.

Daily Integration Check-ins: Several times each day, pause and notice, "What am I thinking right now? How does this show up in my body? What does my integrated system need?"

Weekly Pattern Mapping: Once a week, review the thought-body patterns you've noticed and look for themes. What triggers these patterns? How are they trying to protect you? What do they need to feel safe enough to relax?

Monthly Integration Assessment: Use your developing awareness to assess how well your current life supports integrated healing. What relationships, activities, or environments support your new patterns? What might need to change to support your continued integration?

Trauma-Informed Self-Care: If you're working with significant trauma patterns, be gentle with yourself and consider professional support. Integration work can bring up old memories and feelings, and having appropriate support is crucial.

Your Week 4 Action Plan: The Somatic Cognitive Integration Implementation Guide

This week focuses on healing the split between mind and body, developing skills to work with thoughts and physical sensations as one unified system. You'll learn to track integrated patterns, use your body to support mental flexibility, and interrupt stuck loops that developed from early experiences.

Day 1–2: Integrated Pattern Recognition

Morning Thought-Body Scan: Each morning, spend five minutes identifying your current integrated state and ask:

- What's my dominant emotional or mental state right now?
- What thoughts are most prominent?
- Where do I feel these thoughts in my body?
- What's my overall physical posture and energy?

Hourly Integration Tracking: Set six reminders throughout your day. When the alarm sounds, quickly note:

- What am I thinking about right now?
- Where do I feel this mentally in my body?
- Is my body supporting these thoughts or fighting them?
- What's the relationship between my mental and physical state?

Evening Pattern Mapping: Before sleep, create two columns in your journal:

Column 1: Thought Patterns. List the dominant thoughts you noticed.

Column 2: Physical Patterns. Note where and how each thought showed up in your body.

Look for consistent pairings. Do anxiety thoughts always come with shoulder tension? Do self-critical thoughts always pair with chest collapse?

Key Goal: Develop awareness of your unique thought-body integration patterns.

Day 3–4: Somatic Cognitive Restructuring Practice

Real-Time Integration Work: When you notice problematic thought patterns, practice this sequence:

1. **Pause and Acknowledge**: "I notice the thought '[specific thought]' and I feel it in my [body location] as [physical sensation]."

2. **Provide Somatic Support First**: Before trying to change the thought, tend to your body:

- o Breathe into the area of tension or discomfort.
- o Soften muscles that are bracing or holding.
- o Feel your connection to the ground/support.
- o Find an area of your body that feels more neutral or comfortable.

3. From this resourced state, **Engage Cognitive Flexibility**: "I notice this familiar pattern from [childhood/past experience]. Right now, in this moment, I can see that [more balanced perspective]."

Trauma Pattern Identification: Pay special attention to thought-body patterns that might relate to early experiences:

- Hypervigilance: Body scanning + mental threat assessment.
- People-pleasing: Body contraction + thoughts about others' needs
- Self-criticism: Body collapse + internal attack thoughts.
- Catastrophizing: Body activation + mental disaster scenarios.

Integration Journaling: Record your experiences with somatic cognitive restructuring. What works? What feels difficult? How do your thoughts change when your body feels different?

Key Goal: Learn to provide somatic support before engaging in cognitive work.

Day 5–6: Advanced Integration Techniques

Embodied Affirmations: Create affirmations that include both mental and physical components:

- "I am safe" while feeling your feet on the ground, and breathing into your belly.
- "I am worthy" while opening your chest and lengthening your spine.
- "I belong" while softening your face and feeling supported by your chair.

Practice these three times daily, focusing more on the physical feeling than the mental repetition.

Thought-Body Dialogue: Spend ten minutes each day in conversation between your thinking mind and body wisdom. Ask your body, "What do you need when I think these anxious thoughts?" Ask your mind, "What are you trying to protect me from with these worry patterns?" Let each part respond without judgment.

Movement for Mental Flexibility: When stuck in mental loops, try these physical interruptions:

- For anxious thinking: Gentle shaking or stretching.
- For depressive thinking: Opening movements (arms wide, chest expansion).
- For angry thinking: Pushing movements against a wall or vigorous walking.
- For trauma thinking: Grounding movements (feeling your feet, slow motions).

Key Goal: Develop fluency in working with mind and body as one integrated system.

Day 7: Integration and Trauma Pattern Healing

Weekly Integration Review: Look back at your week's observations:

- What thought-body patterns showed up most frequently?
- Which patterns might relate to childhood experiences or trauma?
- What somatic interventions were most effective for shifting thoughts?
- How has your relationship to these patterns changed?

Childhood Pattern Recognition: For each major thought-body pattern you've identified, ask:

- When did I first learn this pattern?
- How did it protect me in childhood?
- What would this pattern need to feel safe enough to relax now?
- How can I honor its protection while also creating new options?

Integration Intention Setting: Based on your week's discoveries, set intentions for continued healing:

- What thought-body patterns are ready to be transformed?
- What daily practices will support your continued integration?
- What relationships or environments support your new patterns?
- How can you be patient and compassionate with patterns that aren't ready to change yet?

Future Self-Visualization: Spend ten minutes imagining yourself with full somatic cognitive integration:

- Your thoughts and body working together harmoniously.

- Trauma patterns transformed into wisdom and resilience.
- Mental flexibility supported by physical groundedness.
- Old protections honored while new patterns flourish.

Weekly Success Metrics

By the end of Week 4, you should be able to:

- Identify at least five specific thought-body pattern pairs in your system.
- Successfully provide somatic support before engaging in cognitive work.
- Use at least three physical interventions to shift mental patterns.
- Recognize how at least two current patterns might relate to childhood experiences.
- Notice increased flexibility in both thinking and physical responses.

Troubleshooting Common Challenges

"I can't feel the connection between thoughts and body." Start with extreme examples. Notice the difference between thinking about something peaceful versus something stressful. The connection will become clearer with practice.

"Working with my body makes my thoughts worse." This sometimes happens when trauma patterns are activated. Go slower, work with smaller pieces, and consider professional support for trauma processing.

"My childhood patterns feel too overwhelming." You don't have to heal everything at once. Work with current patterns and let childhood connections emerge naturally. Professional trauma therapy can provide additional support.

"Nothing seems to interrupt my thought loops." Some patterns are very entrenched and may need professional intervention. Continue with the practices while considering additional support like EMDR, somatic therapy, or trauma-informed counseling.

Guided Somatic Cognitive Integration Session: Healing the Split Between Mind and Body

Allow approximately 25–30 minutes for this complete integration experience. This session may bring up memories or emotions, so ensure you're in a safe space with support available if needed.

Find a position that feels both comfortable and alert. If you're working with trauma patterns, choose a position where you feel as safe as possible—perhaps sitting with your back supported, feet on the ground, in a familiar space where you won't be interrupted.

Take a moment to acknowledge the courage it takes to work with the intersection of mind and body, especially if you're carrying patterns from difficult early experiences. This work is an act of profound self-care and healing, honoring both the protection these patterns have provided and your readiness to create new possibilities.

Begin with several natural breaths, noticing that your breath connects your mind and body with each inhale and exhale. Your breath is always available as a bridge between thinking and feeling, between past and present, and between protection and possibility.

Moving Through the Shadows

Let's start by creating a foundation of safety and resources. Place one hand on your heart and one on your belly, feeling the connection between these two centers of wisdom. Your heart holds both emotional wisdom and physical rhythm. Your belly holds both intuitive knowing and nervous system regulation.

Bring to mind a memory of feeling genuinely safe and cared for. This might be with a person, in a place in nature, or even a moment of feeling proud of yourself. Don't just think about this memory—let your body remember it. Notice how your breathing changes, how your muscles soften, and how your nervous system settles when you connect with this sense of safety.

This resource state is always available to you, even when working with difficult patterns. You can return to this feeling of safety at any point during this practice.

Now, let's gently explore how thoughts and physical sensations work together in your system. Bring to awareness a mildly challenging situation in your current life—nothing overwhelming, just something that creates some stress or discomfort.

Notice what thoughts arise about the situation. Are they worry thoughts about the future? Are they critical thoughts about yourself or others? Are they protective thoughts about what might go wrong? Simply observe these thoughts without trying to change them.

Now notice where and how these thoughts show up in your body. Do you feel tension, contraction, activation, or perhaps numbness or disconnection? Where specifically do you feel these thoughts physically? In your chest, your stomach, your shoulders, or your jaw?

This is your unique thought-body signature for this particular challenge. Every person experiences this integration differently, and there's no right or wrong way for thoughts and sensations to connect in your system.

Now let's practice working with this integration skillfully. Instead of trying to change your thoughts while your body is in distress, let's first provide some somatic support.

Breathe gently into whatever area of your body is holding tension or discomfort. You're not trying to breathe the sensation away—you're breathing with it, giving it space and oxygen. Let your breath be curious and kind, like a gentle friend offering support.

Feel your connection to the earth beneath you. Let yourself be supported by the chair, the floor, the ground. You don't have to hold yourself up right now—you can let yourself be held.

Find an area of your body that feels more neutral, comfortable, or strong. This might be your feet, your back, your hands, or somewhere else entirely. Let your attention rest in this area of relative comfort or strength.

Now, from this more resourced physical state, notice what happens to your thoughts about the challenging situation. Often, when the body feels more supported, the mind naturally becomes more flexible and creative. You're not forcing positive thoughts—you're creating the conditions where more balanced thinking can emerge.

If self-critical thoughts are present, notice where they live in your body. Often criticism comes with a collapsed chest, rounded shoulders, or contracted abdomen. While breathing into these areas, offer yourself the compassion you'd give a good friend: "I notice these critical thoughts. They're trying to protect me from something. Right now, I can be kind to myself while I figure this out."

If anxious thoughts are dominant, notice their physical signature—perhaps tension in shoulders, rapid heartbeat, or restless energy. While providing somatic support to these areas, acknowledge them by saying, "I notice these worry thoughts. They're trying to prepare me or keep me safe. Right now, I can ground myself while staying appropriately alert."

If angry thoughts are present, feel where that energy lives in your body—maybe jaw clenching, fist tightening, or heat rising. While breathing into these areas, recognize them by saying, "I notice these angry thoughts. They're fighting for something important to me. Right now, I can honor this energy while choosing how to express it wisely."

Let's practice what I call "pendulation" between your old pattern and a new possibility. Focus on your original thought-body pattern for about ten seconds—really feel how the thoughts and physical sensations reinforce each other.

Now shift to your resourced state—the feeling of safety and support, the areas of your body that feel strong or comfortable—for about ten seconds.

Move back and forth between these states several times, each time noticing what shifts or changes. Often, the original pattern may soften, transform, or reveal new information when contrasted with the resourced state.

Let's work with any patterns that might relate to your early experiences. If you notice thought-body patterns that feel very familiar, very old, or very automatic, these might be protective patterns you developed in childhood.

Without trying to analyze or fix these patterns, simply acknowledge them with gratitude: "I notice this familiar pattern. It helped me survive and cope when I was younger. I appreciate how hard it worked to protect me."

From your current adult perspective, with your body feeling as supported as possible, ask this old pattern, "What did you need back then that you didn't get? What do you need now to feel safe enough to relax?"

Listen with curiosity rather than trying to force answers. Sometimes old patterns need to be seen, acknowledged, and appreciated before they're willing to transform.

Now let's imagine your integrated future self—the you that has learned to work skillfully with the connection between mind and body. Visualize yourself moving through challenging situations with your thoughts and physical sensations working together harmoniously.

See yourself noticing thought-body patterns as they arise, providing somatic support when needed, and engaging cognitive flexibility from a grounded, resourced state. Imagine old protective patterns being honored while new, more flexible patterns emerge.

This future self isn't someone who never has difficult thoughts or challenging physical sensations—it's someone who knows how to work skillfully with both, using the wisdom of integration to navigate life's complexities.

As you prepare to complete this practice, take a moment to appreciate your willingness to work with these deep patterns. Integration work requires courage, patience, and self-compassion, especially when working with patterns that developed during difficult times.

Set an intention for how you want to continue this integration work. Perhaps it's to notice thought-body patterns more quickly, to provide somatic support before engaging cognitively, or to treat old protective patterns with more compassion while creating new possibilities.

Remember that this is ongoing work. There will be times when old patterns feel very strong, and that's normal. The goal isn't to eliminate these patterns but to develop more choice in how you work with them, more flexibility in how you respond, and more compassion for the protection they've provided.

Your thoughts and your body are not separate systems that need to be managed independently—they're one integrated intelligence that can work together to support your healing, growth, and authentic expression.

When you're ready, take a deeper breath, gently move your body, and slowly return your attention to the space around you. Carry this sense of integration with you, knowing that you have tools to work skillfully with the beautiful, complex intersection of mind and body that is your unique human experience.

Chapter 8

Week 5: Relational Healing—Connection as Medicine

Breaking the Chains, Building the Bridge

At 35, David stood in his kitchen at 6 a.m., watching his three-year-old daughter Emma play with blocks while his wife Alison fed their six-month-old son. The scene looked perfect—the kind of family morning he'd dreamed of having. But inside his chest, a familiar knot of anxiety was forming. Emma had thrown a tantrum the night before about bedtime, and David's immediate response had been his father's voice: *"Stop that crying right now, or I'll give you something to cry about!"*

He'd caught himself before the words escaped, but the surge of rage that followed the thought terrified him. In that moment, looking down at his small daughter's tear-streaked face, David saw himself at three years old—cowering under his father's towering anger, learning that his emotions were dangerous, that love came with conditions, and that safety meant being invisible.

David had spent years in therapy working to understand his family of origin. His father had been a volatile man who oscillated between emotional absence and explosive rage. His mother had been overwhelmed, using David as her emotional confidant from an early age, burdening him with adult worries while neglecting his own developmental needs. He'd learned to be hypervigilant to others' emotions while suppressing his own, to be the "good boy" who took care of everyone else's needs while his own went unrecognized.

Now, as a father himself, David was determined to break these generational patterns. He read parenting books, practiced patience, and genuinely wanted to be emotionally available for his children. But when stress mounted—when Emma was defiant, when the baby wouldn't stop crying, when Alison was exhausted and snappy—David's nervous system would activate in ways that felt beyond his control.

Sometimes he'd shut down emotionally, becoming cold and distant like his father during the quiet rages. Other times he'd become anxiously overinvolved, trying to fix everyone's emotions like he'd learned to do with his mother. He oscillated between withdrawal and enmeshment, never finding the middle ground of authentic, boundaried connections.

The cruel irony was that his attempts to be a better parent were actually creating the same relational dynamics he'd experienced as a child. His hypervigilance to his children's emotions was teaching them that their feelings were dangerous and needed constant management. His own emotional suppression was modeling the same disconnection from feelings that had wounded him. His people-pleasing patterns were setting up dynamics where his children's needs always came before his own—recreating the same imbalanced relationships that had shaped his childhood.

David was discovering what many parents learn painfully: **You can't give what you didn't receive unless you learn to heal the relational patterns that live in your own nervous system.** His family of origin lived not just in his memories but in his body, in his automatic responses, and in the way he instinctively connected—or failed to connect—with the people he loved most.

What David didn't yet understand was that changing these patterns wasn't just about willpower or better parenting techniques. It required healing the relational template that had been encoded in his nervous system through thousands of interactions with his earliest caregivers. He needed to learn not just how to parent differently, but how to relate differently—to feel his own emotions without becoming overwhelmed, to stay present during conflict, and to give and receive love without losing himself in the process.

The Relational Nervous System: How Connection Shapes Our Emotional Patterns

Human beings are fundamentally relational creatures. Our nervous systems develop in relationships and continue to be regulated through relationships throughout our lives. The emotional patterns you carry—depression, anxiety, anger—weren't formed in isolation. They developed through your earliest relational experiences and continue to be triggered and maintained through your current relationships.

This understanding revolutionizes how we approach emotional healing. **You can't fully heal emotional patterns without**

addressing the relational context in which they exist. Depression isn't just an individual experience of low mood—it's often a relational pattern of disconnection, withdrawal, or learned helplessness in relationships. Anxiety isn't just personal worry—it's frequently a relational pattern of hypervigilance to others' emotions, fear of abandonment, or chronic people-pleasing. Anger isn't just individual frustration—it's often a relational pattern of boundary violations, unmet needs, or power struggles.

Your early caregiving relationships created what attachment researchers call your "internal working model" of relationships—a template that unconsciously guides how you connect with others throughout your life. This template includes beliefs about:

- Whether you're worthy of love and care.
- Whether others are trustworthy and available.
- Whether relationships are safe or dangerous.
- How emotions should be expressed or suppressed in relationships.
- Whether your needs matter and deserve attention.
- How conflict should be handled or avoided.

These patterns live not just in your thoughts but in your nervous system, your body. They're your automatic responses to relational cues. They're activated faster than conscious thought and often feel beyond your control.

Understanding Your Attachment Patterns: The Four Relational Styles

Attachment research has identified four primary patterns of how people connect in relationships, each with its own gifts and challenges:

Secure Attachment (approximately 60 percent of the population)

- Comfortable with both intimacy and independence.
- Able to express needs and emotions directly.
- Can self-regulate and co-regulate effectively.
- Trusts that relationships can weather conflict and difficulty.

Anxious Attachment (approximately 20 percent of the population)

- Craves closeness but fears abandonment.
- Highly attuned to others' emotions and moods.
- Tendency to people-please and suppress own needs.
- Experiences relationships as either wonderful or terrible.

Avoidant Attachment (approximately 20 percent of the population)

- Values independence and self-reliance.
- Uncomfortable with emotional intimacy and vulnerability.
- Tendency to withdraw when others become emotional.
- Believes relationships are ultimately unreliable or burdensome.

Disorganized Attachment (approximately 5 percent of the population)

- Wants close relationships but finds them overwhelming.
- Alternates between anxious and avoidant strategies.
- May have experienced trauma or highly inconsistent caregiving.
- Relationships feel both necessary and dangerous.

Most people have a primary attachment style with elements of others, and these patterns can shift over time with healing and secure relationships.

Are You Recreating Your Family of Origin in Your Current Relationships?

As you consider David's story, reflect on your own relational patterns. Perhaps you recognize:

Anxious Attachment Patterns

- Constantly monitoring others' moods and adjusting your behavior accordingly.
- Difficulty expressing your own needs for fear of pushing others away.
- Feeling responsible for others' emotions and happiness.
- Experiencing relationships as either blissful connection or painful abandonment.

Avoidant Attachment Patterns

- Withdrawing emotionally when relationships become intense or demanding.
- Feeling suffocated by others' emotional needs or expressions.

- Preferring to handle problems alone rather than seeking support.
- Finding it easier to care for others than to receive care.

Disorganized Attachment Patterns

- Wanting close relationships but finding them consistently overwhelming.
- Alternating between clinging and pushing people away.
- Feeling like you don't know how to "do" relationships correctly.
- Experiencing others as both sources of comfort and threat.

Generational Pattern Repetition

- Finding yourself responding to loved ones the way your parents responded to you.
- Recreating the same relationship dynamics you experienced in childhood.
- Passing on emotional patterns you swore you'd never repeat.
- Feeling stuck in cycles despite your best intentions to change.

If these patterns feel familiar, you're discovering how your earliest relationships continue to shape your adult connections.

David's Journey: From Reactive Parenting to Relational Healing

When David first learned about attachment patterns, he felt both validation and despair. Validation because it explained why good intentions weren't enough to change his parenting patterns.

Despair because it seemed like he was doomed to repeat his family's dysfunction despite his best efforts.

David's breakthrough came when he understood that healing relational patterns required working with his own nervous system first. He couldn't give his children the secure attachment he'd never received until he learned to create that security within himself and with other adults.

David began with what might seem like an unlikely practice for a stressed father: he started paying attention to pleasure. Inspired by the ancient Greek philosopher Epicurus, who taught that true pleasure comes from the absence of pain and anxiety, David began noticing moments of genuine enjoyment in his daily life—the taste of his morning coffee, the feeling of his son's weight against his chest, and the sound of Emma's laugh when she wasn't melting down.

"I realized I'd been so focused on being a 'good parent' that I'd forgotten to actually enjoy my children," David reflected. "Epicurus understood that when we're anxious and in pain, we can't experience real pleasure or connection. I had to learn to regulate my own nervous system before I could be truly present with my family."

David practiced "somatic attunement"—learning to notice his own emotional and physical state before responding to his children's needs. When Emma had a tantrum, instead of immediately trying to fix her emotions or becoming overwhelmed by his own, David would take a breath, feel his feet on the ground, and check in with his own nervous system. From this more regulated state, he could stay present with Emma's big feelings without becoming reactive.

The changes were subtle but profound. Instead of the frantic energy of trying to manage everyone's emotions, David began to embody what therapists call a "calm presence." Emma began to trust that her daddy could handle her big feelings without becoming scary or disappearing. Alison noticed that David was more available for adult conversation and connection instead of being constantly preoccupied with managing the family's emotional climate.

Most importantly, David learned to have authentic conversations about his own needs and struggles rather than either suppressing them or expecting Alison to manage them for him. He discovered that when he could acknowledge his own stress and ask for support directly, he was modeling emotional intelligence rather than the suppression and reactivity he'd learned in childhood.

The Four Pillars of Relational Healing

Based on research in attachment theory, interpersonal neurobiology, and relational therapy, healing relationship patterns involves four essential capabilities:

1. Attachment Pattern Recognition: Understanding Your Relational Template

The first step in relational healing is developing awareness of your automatic relational patterns—how you learned to connect, what triggers your attachment system, and how your nervous system responds to different relational dynamics.

Childhood Relationship Mapping. Reflect on your earliest relationships:

- How did your caregivers handle their own emotions?

- What happened when you expressed big feelings as a child?
- How was conflict handled in your family?
- What messages did you receive about your needs and their importance?
- How did you learn to get attention, care, or safety?

Current Pattern Recognition. Notice your automatic responses in relationships:

- Do you tend to over-function (taking care of others' emotions) or under-function (expecting others to manage your emotions)?
- How do you respond when others are upset? Do you try to fix things, withdraw, or become overwhelmed?
- What triggers your attachment system? Abandonment fears, intimacy fears, or both?
- How do you handle conflict? Avoidance, accommodation, or aggression?

Somatic Awareness in Relationships. Learn to track your nervous system responses to different people and relational dynamics:

- Which relationships leave you feeling energized versus drained?
- What physical sensations arise when you're triggered in relationships?
- How does your body respond to different communication styles or emotional expressions?

Why It Works: Awareness of your relational patterns gives you choice in how you respond rather than being at the mercy of automatic reactions.

2. Authentic Expression: Learning to Share Truth Without Overwhelming Others

Many people struggle with two relationship extremes: either suppressing their authentic feelings and needs or expressing them in ways that overwhelm or push others away. Authentic expression involves learning to share your inner experience in ways that invite connection rather than defensive reactions.

Emotional Granularity: Develop a more nuanced vocabulary for your emotional experience. Instead of just "fine," "stressed," or "upset," learn to identify and express specific emotions: "I'm feeling overwhelmed by all the decisions we need to make," or "I notice I'm anxious about how you might react to what I need to say."

"I" Statements from the Body: Practice expressing your experience from your embodied awareness rather than your judgments or interpretations. Instead of "You always interrupt me" (blame), try "I notice my chest tightening when I don't get to finish my thoughts. I need some space to complete what I'm sharing."

Timing and Capacity: Learn to assess both your own and others' capacity for emotional expression. Sometimes the most authentic thing is to say, "I have something important to share with you, and I want to make sure we both have the capacity for this conversation."

Graduated Expression: Practice sharing your inner experience in small, manageable doses rather than waiting until emotions are overwhelming and then flooding others with intensity.

Why It Works: When you can express your authentic experience without overwhelming others, you create the conditions for genuine intimacy and understanding.

3. Boundary Intelligence: Using Body Awareness to Set Relational Limits

Healthy boundaries aren't walls that keep people out—they're permeable membranes that let in what nourishes you and keep out what depletes you. Many people with difficult childhoods never learned how to sense and maintain healthy boundaries, leading to either rigid walls or no boundaries at all.

Somatic Boundary Sensing. Learn to use your body as a boundary detection system:

- What physical sensations arise when someone is asking too much of you?
- How does your body feel when you're about to say yes to something you don't want to do?
- What happens in your nervous system when others are sharing more than you have the capacity to hold?

Energy Management. Practice distinguishing between your own and other people's emotional energy:

- Whose anxiety am I carrying right now?
- Am I trying to manage emotions that aren't mine to manage?
- What would it feel like to give back emotional responsibility that doesn't belong to me?

Boundary Setting with Compassion. Learn to set limits in ways that honor both your needs and your care for others:

- "I care about what you're going through, and I don't have the emotional capacity to help problem-solve right now."
- "I notice I'm feeling overwhelmed by the intensity of this conversation. Can we take a break and come back to this when we're both more regulated?"

Receiving Care and Support. Practice letting others contribute to your well-being without feeling guilty or indebted:

- Notice resistance to receiving help or support.
- Practice saying "Thank you" instead of "I'm sorry" when others offer care.
- Learn to ask for what you need directly rather than hoping others will guess.

Why It Works: Clear, compassionate boundaries create safety for authentic relationships and prevent the resentment that builds when needs and limits aren't honored.

4. Co-Regulation Skills: Creating Relationships That Support Nervous System Balance

Co-regulation is the process by which regulated nervous systems help dysregulated nervous systems return to balance. This is how infants learn to self-regulate through their caregivers' calm presence, and it remains important throughout our lives.

Offering Co-Regulation. Learn to be a regulating presence for others without taking responsibility for their emotions:

- Practice staying grounded in your own body while others are activated.
- Offer a calm presence without trying to fix or change others' emotional states.

- Use your breath and nervous system state to create a field of safety.

Seeking Co-Regulation. Learn to identify and connect with people whose presence helps regulate your nervous system:

- Notice which relationships leave you feeling more centered and grounded.
- Practice asking for the specific type of support that helps you regulate.
- Allow yourself to be soothed by others' calm presence without shame.

Environmental Co-Regulation. Create physical environments that support nervous system balance:

- Design your living spaces to promote calm and connection.
- Use lighting, sound, and scent to create regulatory environments.
- Spend time in nature, which naturally supports nervous system regulation.

Pleasure and Connection. Following Epicurus's wisdom about true pleasure, prioritize activities and relationships that bring genuine joy rather than just stimulation or distraction:

- Notice the difference between superficial pleasure and deep satisfaction.
- Cultivate relationships and activities that feed your soul rather than just fill time.
- Practice savoring moments of genuine connection and joy.

Why It Works: When you can both offer and receive co-regulation, relationships become sources of healing and resilience rather than additional stress.

Applying Relational Healing to David's Family Life

As David developed these relational healing skills, the entire dynamic of his family shifted. Instead of the anxious hypervigilance that had characterized his early parenting, David learned to embody what secure parents naturally provide: a calm, attuned presence that can hold space for big emotions without becoming reactive.

When Emma had tantrums, David practiced staying in his own regulated nervous system state while offering co-regulation through his presence. Instead of trying to stop her crying or becoming overwhelmed by his own activation, he would breathe deeply, feel his feet on the ground, and offer a steady, calm presence. "It's okay to have big feelings, sweetheart. Daddy's right here."

His relationship with Alison deepened as he learned to express his own needs and struggles directly rather than either suppressing them or expecting her to manage them. When he felt overwhelmed by parenting responsibilities, instead of withdrawing or becoming irritable, he learned to say, "I'm feeling maxed out and need some support. Can we problem-solve this together?"

Most importantly, David began to experience genuine pleasure in his family relationships. Following Epicurus's teaching that true pleasure comes from the absence of anxiety and pain, David noticed that as his nervous system became more regulated, he could actually enjoy his children's laughter, appreciate quiet moments with Alison, and feel gratitude for the family life he was creating.

"I realized that my hypervigilance and people-pleasing weren't actually helping my family—they were keeping me from being truly present," David reflected. "When I learned to regulate my own nervous system and express my authentic needs, I could finally give my children what I'd never received: a parent who was genuinely emotionally available."

The Generational Healing Potential of Relational Work

Perhaps the most profound aspect of relational healing is its potential to break generational patterns and create new templates for future relationships. When you heal your own attachment patterns, you're not just improving your current relationships—you're changing the relational legacy you pass on to the next generation.

David's children were learning through thousands of daily interactions that:

- Emotions are safe to feel and express.
- Adults can handle children's big feelings without becoming overwhelmed.
- Relationships can weather conflict and repair.
- People's needs matter and deserve attention.
- Love doesn't have to be earned through perfect behavior.

This is how secure attachment is created—not through perfect parenting, but through consistent, attuned, regulated presence that communicates safety and worth. David was literally rewiring his children's developing nervous systems to expect relationships to be sources of safety rather than danger.

Building Your Relational Healing Practice

Developing secure relational patterns requires practice, patience, and often support from others who embody the security you're learning to create. Remember that these patterns developed over years and may take time to heal—be compassionate with yourself in this process.

Daily Relational Check-ins: Notice your relational patterns throughout the day. How do you respond to others' emotions? What triggers your attachment system? How do you express your own needs?

Weekly Relationship Review: Reflect on your significant relationships. Which ones support your growth and regulation? Which ones trigger old patterns? How can you bring more authenticity and boundaries to challenging relationships?

Monthly Attachment Assessment: Use your growing awareness to evaluate how your relational patterns are shifting. Are you becoming more secure in your attachments? What old patterns are ready to be released?

Pleasure and Connection Practice: Following Epicurus's wisdom, regularly assess whether your relationships bring genuine joy and satisfaction or primarily stress and obligation. Prioritize connections that nourish your authentic self.

Your Week 5 Action Plan: The Relational Healing Implementation Guide

This week focuses on transforming the relationship patterns that maintain emotional suffering. You'll explore your attachment style, practice authentic expression, develop boundary intelligence, and learn to create relationships that support rather than trigger dysregulation.

Day 1–2: Attachment Pattern Recognition and Family of Origin Exploration

Childhood Relationship Mapping. Spend thirty minutes journaling about your earliest relational experiences:

- How did each parent/caregiver handle their own emotions?
- What happened when you expressed big feelings (sadness, anger, fear, excitement)?
- How was conflict handled in your family?
- What messages did you receive about your needs, wants, and feelings?
- How did you learn to get attention, care, comfort, or safety?
- What roles did you play in the family system (caretaker, peacemaker, rebel, invisible child)?

Current Attachment Style Assessment. Reflect on your adult relationship patterns:

- Do you tend toward anxious attachment (fear of abandonment, people-pleasing, hyper-focusing on other people's moods)?
- Are you avoidant leaning (prefer independence, uncomfortable with emotional intimacy, withdraw when others get emotional)?
- Do you experience disorganized patterns (want closeness but find it overwhelming, alternate between clinging and pushing away)?

- What triggers activate your attachment system most strongly?

Relational Body Mapping. Throughout these two days, notice your physical responses in different relationships:

- Which people make your body feel relaxed and open?
- Which relationships create tension, activation, or shutdown in your nervous system?
- What physical sensations arise when you're triggered in relationships?
- How does your body respond to different communication styles?

Key Goal: Develop awareness of your inherited relational patterns and current attachment responses.

Day 3–4: Authentic Expression Practice

Emotional Granularity Development. Instead of general terms like "fine," "stressed," or "upset," practice identifying specific emotions:

- Create a list of 20+ specific emotion words.
- Throughout the day, practice internal emotional precision: "I'm feeling overwhelmed by decisions" rather than "I'm stressed."
- Notice how different emotions feel in your body.

"I" Statement Practice. Transform blame or judgment statements into authentic expression. Practice these conversions:

From: "You never listen to me."

To: "I notice my chest tightening when I don't feel heard. I need some space to finish sharing my thoughts."

From: "You're being too sensitive."

To: "I notice I'm feeling overwhelmed by the intensity of this conversation. Can we take a breath together?"

Graduated Sharing Exercise. Practice sharing your inner experience in small, manageable doses:

- Choose a safe relationship to practice with.
- Share one authentic feeling or need per day.
- Notice your impulse to either overshare or undershare.
- Observe how others respond to your authentic expression.

Capacity Assessment. Before important conversations, practice checking both your own and others' emotional capacity:

- "I have something I'd like to share with you. Do you have the capacity for a deeper conversation right now?"
- "I noticing I'm feeling activated. I need a few minutes to settle before we continue this discussion."

Key Goal: Learn to express your authentic experience in ways that invite connection rather than defensiveness.

Day 5–6: Boundary Intelligence and Energy Management

Somatic Boundary Sensing. Practice using your body as a boundary detection system:

- Throughout the day, notice physical sensations that might indicate boundary violations.
- What happens in your body when someone asks too much of you?
- How does it feel when you're about to say yes to something you don't want to do?

- What sensations arise when others share more than you have the capacity to hold?

Energy Ownership Exercise. Practice distinguishing between your own and other people's emotional energy:

- When you feel anxious ask, "Is this anxiety mine, or am I picking it up from someone else?"
- When others share problems, notice if you automatically try to solve or fix them.
- Practice giving back emotional responsibility. "I notice I've been carrying worry about your situation. I care about you, and I'm giving this worry back to you."

Compassionate Boundary Setting. Practice setting limits that honor both your needs and your care for others:

- "I love you, but I don't have the capacity to process this with you right now."
- "I want to support you, but I need to take care of my own emotional state first."
- "I notice I'm feeling overwhelmed. Can we pause this conversation and come back to it when we're both more regulated?"

Receiving Practice. Challenge patterns of over-giving by practicing receiving:

- Accept compliments without deflecting.
- Let others contribute to your well-being without feeling guilty.
- Ask for specific support when you need it.
- Practice saying "Thank you" instead of "I'm sorry" when others offer help.

Key Goal: Develop body-based awareness of healthy boundaries and practice maintaining them with compassion.

Day 7: Co-Regulation and Pleasure-Based Connection

Co-Regulation Offering Practice. Practice being a calming presence for others without taking responsibility for their emotions:

- When others are activated, focus on staying grounded in your own body.
- Offer a calm presence without trying to fix or change their emotional state.
- Use your breath and posture to create a field of safety.
- Practice phrases like "I'm here with you" or "You're not alone in this."

Co-Regulation Seeking. Identify and connect with people whose presence helps regulate your nervous system:

- Spend time with someone whose calm presence helps you feel more centered.
- Practice asking for the specific type of support that helps you regulate.
- Allow yourself to be soothed by other people's presence without shame or guilt.

Pleasure and Connection Assessment. Following the wisdom of Epicurus about genuine pleasure:

- Review your relationships: Which ones bring genuine joy versus obligation or drama?
- Notice activities you do with others. Which ones create real satisfaction versus just stimulation?

- Practice savoring moments of authentic connection and pleasure.
- Identify one relationship or activity that feeds your soul and commit to prioritizing it.

Weekly Integration. Reflect on your week's relational discoveries:

- What patterns from your family of origin showed up this week?
- How did authentic expression feel? What responses did you receive?
- What did you learn about your boundaries and energy management?
- Which relationships support your nervous system regulation versus triggering dysregulation?

Weekly Success Metrics

By the end of Week 5, you should be able to:

- Identify your primary attachment style and key triggers.
- Express at least one authentic feeling or need per day.
- Recognize boundary violations through body awareness.
- Use at least one co-regulation skill with others.
- Distinguish between relationships that support versus drain your nervous system.

Troubleshooting Common Challenges

"I don't know what I'm feeling or needing." This is common for people with childhood emotional neglect. Start with physical sensations and basic needs (tired, hungry, overwhelmed, need space, need connection). Emotional awareness develops with practice.

"People react badly when I express my needs." Some people in your life may be invested in your old patterns. Start practicing with safer relationships. Remember that others' reactions often reflect their own attachment patterns, not your worth.

"I feel guilty setting boundaries." Guilt often signals that you're changing patterns that served your family system. Boundaries protect relationships by preventing resentment and maintaining your capacity to show up authentically.

"I don't have any secure relationships to practice with." Consider therapy, support groups, or community activities where you can practice relational skills. Even brief interactions with regulated people (kind cashiers, friendly neighbors) can provide co-regulation.

Guided Relational Healing Session: Creating a Secure Connection Within Yourself

Allow approximately 25–30 minutes for this relational healing experience. This practice focuses on developing internal security that supports healthier external relationships.

Find a comfortable position where you feel both supported and alert. Since this practice involves exploring relational patterns, choose a space where you feel emotionally safe and won't be interrupted. You might sit with your back against a wall or in a chair that feels sturdy and supportive.

Take a moment to acknowledge the courage it takes to explore relational patterns, especially if you're carrying wounds from early relationships. This work is an act of love—love for yourself, for your current relationships, and for any children or future generations who will benefit from the healing you're doing.

Begin with several natural breaths, feeling your body's connection to support. Notice that even when you're alone, you're in a relationship—with the earth that holds you, with the air that sustains you, and with your own body that has been your faithful companion through every relationship you've ever had.

Let's start by creating an internal foundation of security. Place one hand on your heart and one on your belly, connecting with these two centers of relational wisdom. Your heart holds your capacity for connection, empathy, and love. Your belly houses your intuitive knowing about safety, boundaries, and authentic needs.

Bring to mind a memory of feeling genuinely safe and cared for in a relationship. This might be with a person, a pet, or even a moment of feeling proud of how you showed up in a relationship. If you can't find a memory from your past, imagine what such an experience would feel like—being seen, accepted, and valued exactly as you are.

Don't just think about this experience—let your body remember or imagine what a secure relationship feels like. Notice how your breathing changes, how your muscles soften, and how your nervous system settles when you connect with this sense of relational safety and security.

This feeling of secure connection is your birthright. It's available to you even when current relationships are challenging, even when you're learning to heal old patterns. You can cultivate this security within yourself and bring it to all your relationships.

Now let's gently explore your relational patterns with curiosity and compassion. Bring to awareness a current relationship that sometimes triggers difficult feelings—perhaps anxiety, anger, or sadness. Choose something manageable for this practice, not your most challenging relationship.

Notice what happens in your body when you think about this relationship. Do you feel tension, activation, contraction, or perhaps numbness? Where specifically do you feel the relational trigger in your physical body?

Without trying to fix or change these sensations, simply acknowledge them with kindness: "I notice this familiar pattern arising. This is how my nervous system learned to respond in relationships. These responses once protected me."

Now, instead of focusing on the other person in this relationship, turn your attention to your own relational patterns. Ask yourself with genuine curiosity:

- Do I tend to become anxious about losing this person's approval or connection?
- Do I withdraw or shut down when this relationship becomes intense?
- Do I try to manage this person's emotions or take responsibility for their happiness?
- Do I lose touch with my own needs and boundaries in this relationship?

Whatever patterns you notice, greet them with appreciation rather than judgment. These patterns developed for good reasons—they helped you survive and cope in your earliest relationships. They deserve gratitude even as you're learning new ways of connecting.

Now let's practice what secure attachment feels like in your body. From your current position, imagine that you have an invisible tether connecting you to an infinitely loving and secure presence.

This might be a spiritual connection, a sense of universal love, or simply your own adult capacity for self-care and wisdom.

Feel this secure base supporting you. From this connection, you can venture into relationships without losing yourself. When relationships become challenging, you can return to this secure base to restore your balance and clarity.

Practice this with your triggering relationship. Imagine interacting with this person while staying connected to your secure base. How might you show up differently? What would you express? What boundaries would you maintain? How would you offer love without losing yourself?

Let's work with authentic expression. Think of something you've been wanting to say to someone important to you—perhaps a need you have, a feeling you've been suppressing, or an appreciation you haven't shared.

Instead of rehearsing the words in your head, drop into your body and feel what wants to be expressed. What does this authentic expression feel like in your chest, your throat, and your belly? Let the words arise from your embodied truth rather than from your thoughts about what you should say.

Practice expressing this authentic communication to the person in your imagination, staying connected to your secure base and breathing into your body. Notice that authentic expression doesn't require the other person to respond in any particular way—it simply requires you to honor your own truth.

Now let's explore healthy boundaries. Imagine a gentle but clear boundary around your body—perhaps like a semi-permeable membrane that lets in what nourishes you and keeps out what depletes you.

Practice saying to yourself, "I am responsible for my own emotions and well-being. I care about others, but I am not responsible for managing their emotional states. I can offer love and support while maintaining my own center."

Feel how this boundary supports rather than separates you from others. Healthy boundaries don't cut you off from connection—they make authentic connection possible by protecting your capacity to show up fully.

Let's practice co-regulation—both offering and receiving it. Imagine someone you care about who is going through a difficult time. Instead of trying to fix their problem or take away their pain, practice offering your calm, grounded presence.

Breathe deeply and imagine your regulated nervous system creating a field of safety around them. You're not trying to change their experience—you're simply offering the gift of your presence and stability.

Now reverse the practice. Imagine yourself going through a challenging time and someone offering you this same kind of regulated, present support. Practice receiving this gift without feeling guilty or indebted. Let yourself be held by another's calm presence.

This is the dance of a secure relationship—offering and receiving support, maintaining individual integrity while creating connection, and being authentically yourself while staying open to others.

Following the wisdom of Epicurus, let's end by connecting with genuine pleasure in relationship. Bring to mind a relationship or relational experience that brings you authentic joy—not just excitement or stimulation, but deep satisfaction and contentment.

This might be a conversation where you felt truly seen and understood, a moment of shared laughter, an experience of giving or receiving care, or simply the pleasure of being yourself with someone who accepts you completely.

Let yourself fully experience this relational pleasure in your body. Notice how different this feels from relationships based on anxiety, obligation, or people-pleasing. This is what you're moving toward—relationships that feed your soul rather than drain your energy.

Set an intention for how you want to show up in your relationships going forward. Perhaps it's to express your authentic needs more directly, to maintain boundaries with more compassion, to offer presence without trying to fix, or to seek out relationships that support your growth and joy.

Imagine yourself moving through your daily relationships with this intention—staying connected to your secure base, expressing your truth, maintaining loving boundaries, and offering and receiving co-regulation. See yourself as someone who can love fully while staying centered in your own integrity.

As you prepare to complete this practice, take a moment to appreciate the relational courage you're developing. It takes bravery to break generational patterns, to risk authentic expression, and to maintain boundaries while staying open to love.

Remember that relational healing is ongoing work. There will be times when old patterns feel very strong, and that's normal. The goal isn't to have perfect relationships but to develop the capacity for increasingly secure, authentic, and mutually nourishing connections.

Your relationships are not just personal—they're part of the healing of collective relational trauma.

Chapter 9

Week 6: Meaning and Purpose Integration— Connecting to Something Larger

The Hollow Victory and the Search for Soul

At 42, Marcus had achieved everything he thought he wanted. As a successful architect, he designed buildings that shaped city skylines, earned six figures, and received professional recognition. His social media showed the perfect life—expensive dinners, vacation photos, and career achievements. But standing in his pristine downtown loft at 3 a.m., staring out at the city lights, Marcus felt completely empty inside.

The depression had crept in slowly, like fog rolling over a landscape. At first, he attributed it to work stress or relationship issues. But as he achieved more professional success, the emptiness only deepened. The anxiety about his next project, his performance reviews, and his reputation felt increasingly meaningless. The anger that would surge when clients changed designs or colleagues received credit felt disproportionate and exhausting.

"I have everything I'm supposed to want," Marcus would tell himself, "so why do I feel like I'm dying inside?"

The turning point came during a panic attack in his office. As his chest tightened and his breathing became shallow, Marcus looked around at his awards, his expensive furniture, and his portfolio of impressive buildings and realized he felt no connection to any of it. These achievements belonged to someone he had created to be successful, but they had nothing to do with who he actually was or what truly mattered to him.

Marcus began to remember a different version of himself—the child who spent hours building elaborate structures with LEGOs, not because anyone was watching or evaluating, but because the act of creating brought him pure joy. The teenager who volunteered at Habitat for Humanity, feeling deeply moved by helping families have homes. The young man who dreamed of designing community centers and schools that would nurture human connection and growth.

Somewhere along the way, Marcus had traded his authentic calling for external validation. He had learned to measure success by others' standards rather than his own sense of meaning and purpose. His body was responding to this betrayal of his authentic self with depression, anxiety, and anger—emotions that were trying to redirect him toward what truly mattered.

What Marcus didn't yet understand was that his emotional suffering wasn't a sign of mental illness—it was his soul's rebellion against a life that had become disconnected from meaning. His depression wasn't random sadness; it was grief for the dreams he'd abandoned. His anxiety wasn't just stress; it was his system's alarm about living inauthentically. His anger wasn't just irritation; it was his authentic self fighting for recognition and expression.

Marcus was discovering what researchers call "spiritual emergency"—the crisis that occurs when our outer life becomes drastically misaligned with our inner values and authentic purpose. His emotional symptoms were actually pointing him toward the healing he most needed: reconnecting with what gave his life genuine meaning and purpose.

The Crisis of Meaninglessness: When Success Becomes Suffering

In our achievement-oriented culture, many people experience what philosophers call "existential emptiness"—the sense that despite external success, life feels hollow, pointless, or devoid of real significance. This disconnection from meaning is one of the most common underlying factors in depression, anxiety, and chronic anger.

Depression and Meaninglessness: Depression often arises when life feels pointless or when we're living in ways that betray our authentic values. The heaviness and lack of motivation that characterize depression can be your psyche's way of refusing to engage with activities that don't align with your deeper purpose.

Anxiety and Purpose Disconnection: Anxiety frequently intensifies when we're pursuing goals that don't genuinely matter to us or when we're living according to others' expectations rather than our own values. The nervous system activation of anxiety can signal that we're moving in directions that don't serve our authentic self.

Anger and Values Violation: Chronic anger often emerges when our deepest values are being violated—either by others or by our own choices. The mobilized energy of anger can be our authentic self fighting for recognition and expression.

This understanding revolutionizes how we approach emotional healing. Instead of treating depression, anxiety, and anger as symptoms to eliminate, we can recognize them as messengers pointing us toward the meaning and purpose our souls are craving.

Understanding Eudaimonic vs. Hedonic Well-Being

Ancient Greek philosophy distinguished between two types of happiness that remain relevant for modern emotional healing:

Hedonic Well-Being. Pleasure-seeking and pain avoidance:

- Focus on feeling good and avoiding discomfort.
- Short-term satisfaction and immediate gratification.
- External sources of validation and pleasure.
- Often leads to addiction, compulsion, or emptiness when pleasure fades.

Eudaimonic Well-Being. Living according to your authentic self and values:

- Focus on meaning, purpose, and authentic expression.
- Long-term fulfillment that persists through difficulties.
- Internal sources of satisfaction and worth.
- Creates resilience and sustainable happiness.

Research consistently shows that people who prioritize eudaimonic well-being experience significantly less depression, anxiety, and anger, even during challenging life circumstances. When your life is aligned with your authentic values and purpose, you have an internal compass that guides you through difficulties.

Are You Living Someone Else's Definition of Success?

As you consider Marcus's story, reflect on your own relationship with meaning and purpose. Perhaps you recognize:

Signs of Meaning Disconnection:
- Achieving goals that feel empty once accomplished.
- Success that brings recognition but no internal satisfaction.
- Daily activities that feel obligatory rather than meaningful.
- Career or life path chosen to please others rather than express your authentic self.
- Sense that you're "going through the motions" without genuine engagement.

Depression as Meaning-Seeking:
- Lack of motivation for activities that once felt important.
- Sense that nothing you do matters or makes a difference.
- Grief for dreams or paths you abandoned.
- Feeling like you're living someone else's life.
- Exhaustion from pursuing goals that don't align with your values.

Anxiety as Purpose Confusion:
- Worry about whether you're making the "right" choices.
- Fear of disappointing others by following your authentic path.
- Overwhelm from trying to meet expectations that aren't your own.

- Restlessness or dissatisfaction despite external achievements.
- Sense that time is running out to find your "real" purpose.

Anger as Authentic Self-Protection:
- Resentment toward people or systems that prevent authentic expression.
- Frustration with yourself for betraying your own values.
- Rage at societal pressures to conform to others' definitions of success.
- Irritation with activities or relationships that feel meaningless.
- Anger at having "wasted" time pursuing the wrong goals.

If these patterns feel familiar, your emotions may be guiding you toward a more authentic, meaningful way of living.

Marcus's Journey: From Achievement to Authentic Purpose

When Marcus first began exploring meaning and purpose, he felt overwhelmed by the gap between his current life and his authentic values. How could he possibly change a successful career that supported his lifestyle? How could he disappoint family members who were proud of his achievements? How could he start over at 42?

Marcus's breakthrough came when he realized that reconnecting with meaning didn't require dramatic external changes—it required internal alignment that could transform how he approached his existing life. He began with what seemed like a small practice: before starting any project, he would pause and ask, "How can I bring my authentic values to this work?"

Instead of designing buildings purely for profit or prestige, Marcus began focusing on how his architectural work could serve human flourishing. He started incorporating more natural light, community spaces, and sustainable materials. He volunteered his skills for nonprofit organizations, designing community gardens and affordable housing projects.

The changes in his emotional state were dramatic. The depression that had felt so heavy began to lift as Marcus reconnected with the joy of creating spaces that served people's well-being. His anxiety about performance and recognition decreased as he focused on alignment with his values rather than external validation. His anger transformed from destructive frustration into constructive energy for advocating for sustainable and community-centered design.

"I realized I didn't have to change my entire career," Marcus reflected. "I had to change my relationship to my career. When I started approaching architecture as a way to serve something larger than myself, everything shifted. The same work that had felt meaningless became deeply fulfilling."

Marcus also began exploring "micro-purposes"—small daily actions that aligned with his values even when his bigger life circumstances were still in transition. He mentored young architecture students, volunteered with Habitat for Humanity on weekends, and incorporated meditation and nature connection into his daily routine.

Most importantly, Marcus learned to distinguish between his ego's definition of success (recognition, money, status) and his soul's definition of fulfillment (service, creativity, authentic expression). This distinction became his compass for making decisions both large and small.

The Four Foundations of Meaning and Purpose Integration

Based on research in positive psychology, existential therapy, and spiritual traditions, developing sustainable meaning and purpose involves four essential practices:

1. Values Embodiment: Connecting to Your Deepest Values Through Somatic Awareness

Your authentic values aren't just mental concepts—they live in your body as felt senses of rightness, alignment, and energy. Learning to recognize and embody your values somatically helps you make decisions from your authentic self rather than from external expectations.

Somatic Values Discovery. Instead of thinking your way to your values, practice feeling them:

- When have you felt most alive and authentic? What values were you expressing?
- What activities or experiences make your body feel energized rather than drained?
- What causes or issues create a physical sense of "Yes, this matters" in your system?
- What injustices or problems create activation that wants to be channeled into action?

Values as Body Compass. Learn to use your physical responses as guidance for values-aligned choices:

- When considering decisions, notice your body's response to different options.
- What creates expansion, energy, and aliveness versus contraction and depletion?

- Practice making small daily choices based on what feels most aligned in your body.
- Use physical sensations to detect when you're betraying your own values.

Embodied Values Practices. Create regular practices that help you feel your values in your body:

- Take walks in nature if you value connection to the earth.
- Engage in creative expression if you value beauty and authenticity.
- Volunteer or serve others if you value compassion and justice.
- Spend time in meaningful conversation if you value deep connection.

Why It Works: When values are embodied rather than just conceptual, they become reliable guides for authentic living that your nervous system recognizes and supports.

2. Purpose Practices: Small, Meaningful Actions That Align with Your Authentic Self

Purpose doesn't have to be one grand calling—it can be woven into daily life through small, meaningful actions that align with your authentic self. These "micro-purposes" create a sense of meaning even when your larger life circumstances are in transition.

Daily Purpose Practices. Identify small ways to express your authentic self and values every day:

- If you value creativity, commit to one creative act daily (drawing, writing, cooking).

- If you value service, find small ways to help others (listening, volunteering, random kindness).
- If you value learning, engage with new ideas or skills regularly.
- If you value connection, prioritize authentic conversations and relationships.

Work Purpose Integration. Find ways to bring meaning to existing responsibilities:

- How can your current job serve your values, even in small ways?
- What aspects of your work align with your authentic self?
- How can you approach obligations in ways that express your values?
- What small changes could make your work feel more meaningful?

Purpose Experimentation. Try different expressions of meaning without committing to major life changes:

- Volunteer with organizations that align with your values.
- Take classes or workshops in areas that interest you.
- Engage in creative projects or hobbies that bring joy.
- Participate in community activities or causes you care about.

Legacy Practices. Regularly connect with how your actions contribute to something larger:

- How do your daily choices impact future generations?
- What kind of influence do you want to have on others?
- How can your unique gifts serve the healing of the world?
- What would you want to be remembered for?

Why It Works: Small, consistent purpose practices create sustainable meaning that doesn't depend on dramatic life changes or external validation.

3. Service Integration: Contributing to Something Larger Than Yourself

Research consistently shows that contributing to something beyond our personal concerns is one of the most reliable sources of meaning and emotional well-being. Service doesn't have to be formal volunteering—it can be any way you use your unique gifts to benefit others or the world.

Gift-Based Service. Identify your natural talents and find ways to share them:

- What do people consistently come to you for help with?
- What activities feel effortless and energizing to you?
- How can you use your professional skills for service?
- What wisdom have you gained from your struggles that could help others?

Concentric Circles of Service. Start with service that feels manageable and expand gradually:

- Family and friends: How can you show up more fully for people you love?
- Community: What needs in your immediate community call to you?
- Society: What larger social issues align with your values and abilities?
- Planet: How can your choices and actions support environmental and global wellbeing?

Service as Spiritual Practice. Approach service as a way of connecting with the sacred:

- See service as an opportunity to express love and compassion.
- Practice giving without attachment to outcomes or recognition.
- Use service as a way to develop humility and interconnection.
- Let service be a form of prayer or meditation in action.

Advocacy and Justice. Channel your anger and passion into constructive action:

- What injustices activate your anger in ways that call for a response?
- How can you use your voice, resources, or skills to advocate for change?
- What systems or structures need your unique perspective or talents?
- How can you transform personal pain into collective healing?

Why It Works: Service connects us to our interdependence with all life, providing perspective on personal problems and creating sustainable sources of meaning.

4. Spiritual Somatic Practices: Connecting to the Sacred Through Embodied Experience

Spirituality doesn't require specific religious beliefs—it involves connecting to whatever you experience as sacred, transcendent, or larger than your individual ego. Somatic spiritual practices help you feel this connection in your body rather than just thinking about it.

Nature Connection. Use the natural world as a gateway to the sacred:

- Spend time in nature regularly, noticing your body's response to natural beauty.
- Practice feeling your connection to the earth, sky, plants, and animals.
- Let nature teach you about cycles, impermanence, and interconnection.
- Use natural elements (water, fire, earth, air) in contemplative practices.

Embodied Prayer or Meditation. Develop practices that connect mind, body, and spirit:

- Create movement-based spiritual practices (walking meditation, dance, yoga).
- Use breathwork as a bridge between physical and spiritual experience.
- Practice gratitude as a full-body experience rather than just mental acknowledgment.
- Develop rituals that mark transitions and sacred moments.

Sacred Activism. Approach your service and advocacy as spiritual practice:

- See your work for justice and healing as sacred calling.
- Practice bringing spiritual qualities (compassion, wisdom, patience) to activism.
- Let your engagement with world problems deepen rather than separate you from spiritual connection.
- Use meditation and contemplation to sustain your ability to serve.

Meaning-Making Practices. Develop regular practices for reflecting on life's deeper significance:

- Journal about experiences of transcendence, beauty, or connection.
- Create artistic expressions of your spiritual experiences.
- Engage with wisdom traditions that resonate with your experience.
- Practice seeing ordinary moments as opportunities for sacred connection.

Why It Works: Spiritual practices provide perspective on personal suffering and connect us to sources of meaning that transcend individual circumstances.

Applying Meaning Integration to Marcus's Transformation

As Marcus developed these meaning and purpose practices, his entire relationship with his emotional life transformed. The depression that had felt like a heavy blanket began to lift as he reconnected with work that aligned with his values. His designs began incorporating community spaces, sustainable materials, and accessibility features that reflected his authentic caring for human well-being.

His anxiety about professional success decreased as he focused on internal alignment rather than external validation. When clients criticized his more values-based designs, Marcus could stay centered because he knew his work was serving something larger than just profit or recognition.

Most dramatically, his anger transformed from destructive frustration into constructive passion. Instead of being angry at clients and colleagues, Marcus channeled his anger into advocacy for sustainable design practices and affordable housing initiatives. His anger became fuel for positive change rather than a source of relationship conflict.

Marcus began volunteering with organizations that built community gardens and affordable housing, using his professional skills in service of his values. He mentored young architects interested in socially conscious design. He incorporated meditation and nature connection into his daily routine, finding spiritual meaning in both solitude and service.

"I realized that my depression, anxiety, and anger weren't signs that something was wrong with me," Marcus reflected. "They were signs that something was wrong with how I was living. When I started aligning my life with what actually mattered to me, these emotions became allies instead of enemies. My depression taught me to slow down and reconsider my priorities. My anxiety pushed me to question whether I was living authentically. My anger gave me energy to advocate for what I believed in."

The Neuroscience of Meaning: How Purpose Heals the Brain

Research in neuroscience shows that living with meaning and purpose creates measurable changes in brain structure and function. People who report high levels of purpose show:

- **Increased prefrontal cortex activity**: Better executive function, decision-making, and emotional regulation.
- **Stronger default mode network**: More integrated sense of self and reduced rumination.
- **Enhanced neuroplasticity**: Greater capacity for learning, growth, and recovery from trauma.

- **Improved stress resilience**: Better ability to cope with challenges without becoming overwhelmed.

This neurobiological research confirms what wisdom traditions have long understood: when we live according to our authentic values and contribute to something larger than ourselves, our entire system—mental, emotional, physical, and spiritual—functions more harmoniously.

Building Your Meaning and Purpose Practice

Developing sustainable meaning and purpose is not about finding one perfect calling—it's about cultivating ongoing alignment between your daily life and your deepest values. This alignment can be developed gradually through small, consistent practices.

Daily Meaning Check-Ins: Regularly assess whether your activities align with your values. What felt meaningful today? What felt empty or obligatory? How can you bring more alignment to tomorrow?

Weekly Purpose Practices: Engage in at least one activity each week that serves something larger than your personal concerns. This might be volunteering, creative expression, mentoring, or advocacy.

Monthly Values Assessment: Reflect on whether your major life choices are supporting or undermining your authentic values. What changes might better support your sense of meaning and purpose?

Annual Purpose Review: Take time each year to assess the bigger picture of your life's direction and meaning. How has your understanding of purpose evolved? What new expressions of meaning are calling to you?

Your Week 6 Action Plan: The Meaning and Purpose Integration Implementation Guide

This week focuses on reconnecting with what gives your life authentic meaning and purpose. You'll explore your deepest values, create daily purpose practices, engage in service, and develop spiritual somatic practices that connect you to something larger than individual concerns.

Day 1–2: Values Discovery and Embodiment

Somatic Values Exploration. Instead of thinking your way to your values, practice feeling them in your body:

Life Energy Audit. Reflect on activities and experiences that energize versus drain you:

- What activities make your body feel alive and expansive?
- What causes or issues create a physical sense of "Yes, this matters deeply"?
- When have you felt most authentic and aligned? What values were you expressing?
- What injustices or problems create activation that wants to become constructive action?

Values Body Mapping. For each value you identify, notice how it shows up somatically:

- Where do you feel "justice" in your body when it's honored or violated?
- How does "creativity" feel when you're expressing it versus suppressing it?

- What does "compassion" feel like as a physical experience?
- How does your body respond when "authenticity" is present versus absent?

Daily Values Check-Ins. Throughout these two days, before making decisions (small or large), pause and ask:

- Which choice feels most aligned in my body?
- What creates expansion and energy versus contraction and depletion?
- How can I honor my authentic values in this situation?

Values Embodiment Practices. Choose 2–3 core values and create simple daily practices to embody them:

- If you value creativity, commit to one creative act daily.
- If you value connection, prioritize one meaningful conversation daily.
- If you value justice, take one small action for fairness daily.
- If you value nature, spend time outdoors with conscious appreciation daily.

Key Goal: Identify your core values through somatic awareness and begin embodying them daily.

Day 3–4: Purpose Practice Development

Current Life Purpose Audit. Examine how much meaning exists in your current activities:

- What aspects of your work/responsibilities align with your values?
- Which daily activities feel meaningful versus obligatory?

- How could you approach existing responsibilities in more purpose-aligned ways?
- What small changes could increase meaning in your current life?

Micro-Purpose Practices. Identify small ways to express purpose daily without major life changes:

- If your value is service, find small ways to help others (listening, volunteering, random kindness).
- If your value is learning, engage with new ideas, skills, or perspectives daily.
- If your value is beauty, create, appreciate, or share something beautiful daily.
- If your value is healing, contribute to wellness for yourself, others, or the planet daily.

Purpose Experimentation. Choose one new activity this week that aligns with your values:

- Volunteer for 2–4 hours with an organization that serves your values.
- Take a class or workshop in something that genuinely interests you.
- Start a creative project that expresses your authentic self.
- Engage in advocacy or community action around an issue you care about.

Work Integration Practice. Find ways to bring your values into existing work/responsibilities:

- How can your current job serve your values, even in small ways?
- What conversations could you have that align with your authentic self?

- How can you approach tasks in ways that express what matters to you?
- What small changes could make your work feel more meaningful?

Key Goal: Create daily micro-purpose practices and experiment with larger purpose expressions.

Day 5–6: Service Integration and Gift-Based Contribution

Gift Inventory. Identify your unique talents and how they could serve others:

- What do people consistently come to you for help with?
- What activities feel effortless and energizing to you?
- What wisdom have you gained from your struggles that could help others?
- How could you use your professional skills for service?

Concentric Circles Service Planning. Design a service that feels sustainable including:

- **Inner Circle (Family/Friends)**: How can you show up more fully for people you love?
- **Community Circle**: What needs in your immediate community call to you?
- **Society Circle**: What larger social issues align with your values and abilities?
- **Planet Circle**: How can your choices support environmental and global well-being?

Service as Spiritual Practice. Approach one act of service this week as sacred practice:

- Choose a service that genuinely aligns with your values rather than obligation.

- Practice giving without attachment to outcomes or recognition.
- Let the service be a form of meditation or prayer in action.
- Notice how service affects your own sense of meaning and connection.

Advocacy Channel Practice. Transform personal pain or anger into constructive action:

- What injustices activate your anger in ways that call for response?
- How can you use your voice, resources, or skills to advocate for change?
- What small action could you take this week toward positive change?
- How can you channel difficult emotions into energy for healing or justice?

Key Goal: Engage in meaningful service that uses your gifts and contributes to something larger than personal concerns.

Day 7: Spiritual Integration and Sacred Connection

Nature Connection Practice: Spend at least thirty minutes in nature as spiritual practice:

- Notice your body's response to natural beauty and wonder.
- Practice feeling your connection to earth, sky, plants, and animals.
- Let nature teach you about cycles, impermanence, and interconnection.
- Use natural elements in contemplative practices (a walking meditation, sitting by water).

Sacred Meaning-Making. Reflect on your week's experiences of meaning and purpose:

- What moments felt most sacred or transcendent?
- How did serving others affect your own sense of well-being?
- What connections did you feel to something larger than yourself?
- How has your relationship with difficult emotions shifted through meaning-focused work?

Embodied Spiritual Practice. Develop a practice that connects body, mind, and spirit:

- Create a movement-based spiritual practice (dance, walking meditation, yoga).
- Use breathwork as a bridge between physical and spiritual experience.
- Practice gratitude as a full-body experience rather than a mental acknowledgment.
- Develop a simple ritual that honors transitions and sacred moments.

Future Purpose Visioning. Imagine your life aligned with authentic meaning and purpose:

- What would your daily life look like if fully aligned with your values?
- How would you contribute your unique gifts to the world's healing?
- What legacy would you want to leave through your choices and actions?
- How would living with authentic purpose affect your emotional well-being?

Integration Planning. Based on your week's discoveries, create sustainable meaning practices:

- What daily micro-purpose practices will you continue?
- How will you maintain connection to service and contribution?
- What spiritual practices support your sense of connection to the sacred?
- How will you use meaning and purpose as medicine for difficult emotions?

Weekly Success Metrics

By the end of Week 6, you should be able to:

- Identify your core values through somatic awareness rather than just mental analysis.
- Practice at least three daily micro-purpose activities that align with your authentic self.
- Engage in meaningful service that uses your gifts to contribute to something larger.
- Use spiritual practices to connect with the sacred through embodied experience.
- Transform difficult emotions into fuel for meaningful action and authentic expression.

Troubleshooting Common Challenges

"I don't know what my purpose is." Purpose doesn't have to be one grand calling. Start with micro-purposes—small daily actions that feel meaningful. Purpose often emerges through engagement rather than contemplation.

"My values conflict with my responsibilities." Start with small ways to honor values within existing circumstances rather than making dramatic changes. Often internal alignment can transform how external responsibilities feel.

"I feel guilty focusing on meaning when I have practical concerns." Meaning and purpose actually support practical well-being by providing motivation, resilience, and direction. They're not luxuries but necessities for sustainable emotional health.

"Service feels overwhelming or obligatory." Choose service that genuinely aligns with your values and interests. Start small and let it grow naturally. Service should energize rather than deplete you when it's truly aligned.

Guided Meaning and Purpose Integration Session: Connecting to Your Sacred Calling

Allow approximately 25–30 minutes for this meaning and purpose integration experience. This practice focuses on connecting with your authentic values and sacred purpose through embodied awareness.

Find a position that feels both grounded and open—perhaps sitting with your spine straight but not rigid, your feet connected to the earth, and your heart open to possibility. Since this practice involves connecting with what's sacred to you, choose a space where you feel emotionally and spiritually safe.

Take a moment to acknowledge the courage it takes to explore meaning and purpose, especially if you've been living according to others' expectations rather than your own authentic calling. This exploration is an act of reverence for your soul's deepest longings and your unique contribution to the world.

Begin with several natural breaths, feeling your connection to the life force that animates all beings. With each breath, you're participating in the same exchange of oxygen and carbon dioxide that connects you to every plant, animal, and person on Earth. You are already part of something infinitely larger than your individual concerns.

Place one hand on your heart and one on your belly, connecting with these centers of wisdom and knowing. Your heart holds your capacity for love, compassion, and values-based living. Your belly houses your intuitive wisdom about what truly matters to you and what your authentic self is called to express.

Let's begin by creating a foundation of sacred connection. Whether you call it God, Universe, Source, Life Force, or simply the mystery of existence itself, take a moment to connect with whatever feels sacred or transcendent to you. This might be a religious connection, a spiritual presence, or simply the awe-inspiring mystery of consciousness and life.

Feel this sacred connection not just as an idea but as a felt presence in your body. Notice how your breathing changes, how your nervous system settles, and how your sense of individual isolation softens when you remember your connection to something infinitely larger than yourself.

Now let's explore your authentic values through somatic awareness. Instead of thinking your way to what should matter to you, let's feel what does matter to you in your body.

Bring to mind a moment when you felt most alive, most authentic, and most like your true self. This might be a moment of creative expression, service to others, connection with nature, or simply being genuinely yourself with someone who loved you completely.

Don't just remember this experience—let your body remember it. Feel the energy, the aliveness, and the sense of rightness that was present in that moment. Notice how your posture changes, how your breathing shifts, and how your entire being responds to remembering authentic alignment.

What values were you expressing in that moment? Was it creativity, compassion, justice, beauty, connection, authenticity, service, or something else entirely? Let the values emerge from your felt experience rather than your thoughts about what should be important to you.

Now think of a time when you felt angry about injustice or wrongness in the world—not petty irritation, but the kind of anger that arises when something you care deeply about is being violated or harmed.

Feel that anger in your body—not to get lost in it, but to understand what it's protecting or fighting for. What values is this anger defending? What does it care so much about that it mobilizes your entire system for action?

This anger is sacred—it's your soul's response to the violation of what you hold dear. It carries information about what you're called to protect, defend, or fight for in this world.

Let's also explore what brings you genuine joy and energy. Bring to mind activities or experiences that make you feel truly alive—not just entertained or distracted, but deeply nourished and energized.

Feel these experiences in your body. Notice the quality of energy they create—the expansion, the lightness, the sense of being fully present and engaged. These experiences point you toward your authentic self and natural gifts.

Now let's connect with your unique contribution to the world's healing. Every person has gifts, perspectives, and experiences that only they can offer. Your struggles have taught you things that can help others navigate similar challenges. Your joys have revealed capacities that can bring light to the world.

Ask yourself, What have I learned from my difficulties that could help others? What comes naturally to me that others seem to struggle with? What do people consistently seek my help with? How has my unique life experience given me wisdom or abilities that could serve others?

Feel the energy of your unique gifts in your body. Notice that when you connect with what you have to offer, your nervous system often feels more regulated, more centered, and more purposeful.

Let's practice what it feels like to live from authentic purpose. Imagine approaching your daily life—your work, your relationships, your challenges—from a place of alignment with your deepest values and authentic gifts.

See yourself making decisions based on what feels most aligned in your body rather than what others expect. Imagine engaging in work that serves something you genuinely care about, even if it's bringing new intention to existing responsibilities.

Visualize yourself contributing your unique gifts to the world's healing in whatever way feels authentic to you—whether through formal service, creative expression, compassionate presence, or simply living as an example of authentic alignment.

Notice how different this feels from living according to external expectations or pursuing goals that don't genuinely matter to you. Feel the energy, the aliveness, and the sense of rightness that comes with authentic purpose.

Now let's connect with the sacred dimension of your purpose. Whether or not you consider yourself religious or spiritual, there's something mysterious and sacred about the fact that you exist, that you have unique gifts to offer, and that your choices and actions ripple out to affect others and future generations.

Feel yourself as part of the ongoing evolution of consciousness, love, and healing on this planet. Your personal healing contributes to collective healing. Your authentic expression gives others permission to be authentic. Your service, however small, participates in the healing of the world.

This isn't a burden—it's a profound gift. You get to participate in something infinitely meaningful simply by being genuinely yourself and offering your unique gifts to life.

Let's end by setting an intention for how you want to live from this sense of meaning and purpose. This doesn't require dramatic external changes—it requires internal alignment that can transform how you approach your existing life.

Perhaps your intention is to make daily decisions based on your authentic values rather than others' expectations. Maybe it's to find small ways to serve something larger than your personal concerns. It might be to approach your current work with a new intention or to prioritize activities that genuinely nourish your soul.

Imagine yourself living with this intention—connected to your values, expressing your authentic gifts, contributing to something larger than yourself. See how this affects your emotional well-being, your relationships, and your sense of vitality and aliveness.

Feel how depression, anxiety, and anger transform when your life is aligned with authentic meaning. Depression lifts when you're engaged with what genuinely matters. Anxiety decreases when you're living according to your own values rather than others' expectations. Anger becomes constructive energy for positive change rather than destructive frustration.

As you prepare to complete this practice, take a moment to appreciate the sacred nature of this exploration. You're not just seeking personal happiness—you're discovering how to offer your unique gifts to the healing and evolution of the world.

Set an intention to carry this sense of meaning and purpose into your daily life. Remember that authentic purpose isn't something you find once and then possess—it's something you reconnect with daily through your choices, your attention, and your willingness to live from your deepest values.

Your life has meaning not because of what you achieve or acquire, but because of who you are and how you choose to show up in the world. Your authentic expression matters. Your unique gifts are needed. Your contribution to the world's healing is sacred and irreplaceable.

When you're ready, take a deeper breath, gently move your body, and slowly return your attention to the space around you. Carry this sense of meaning and purpose with you, knowing that you have touched something sacred—your own authentic calling to contribute to the healing and evolution of life itself.

Chapter 10

Week 7: Integration and Daily Practice—Making Transformation Sustainable

The Weight of Good Intentions and the Power of Small Steps

At 29, Keisha had filled three notebooks with self-help strategies, attended countless workshops, and could recite affirmations in her sleep. As a Black woman navigating corporate America while dealing with depression that seemed to ebb and flow like an unpredictable tide, she'd tried everything: therapy, medication, meditation retreats, juice cleanses, exercise programs, and gratitude practices. Each new approach would work for a while—sometimes weeks, occasionally months—before she'd slip back into the familiar darkness.

The depression wasn't just sadness. It was bone-deep exhaustion that made getting dressed feel like climbing mountains. It was the voice that whispered she wasn't smart enough, wasn't working hard enough, and wasn't strong enough to deserve the success she'd achieved as a marketing director. It was the weight of carrying not just her own struggles but the additional burden of representing her race in predominantly white professional spaces, never being able to show weakness or vulnerability without risking confirmation of harmful stereotypes.

Keisha's latest attempt at transformation had been ambitious: a 5 a.m. workout routine, twenty minutes of meditation, journaling, green smoothies, evening yoga, and weekly therapy sessions. For three weeks, she maintained this schedule with the determination that had carried her through graduate school and into her current position. She felt proud, powerful, like she was finally taking control of her mental health.

Then her workload increased. A major client crisis required 12-hour days and weekend work. Her grandmother was hospitalized. Her apartment's hot water heater broke, requiring time off work for repairs. Life happened, as life does, and Keisha's elaborate self-care routine crumbled.

The guilt was crushing. Not only was she depressed again, but now she felt like a failure at healing from depression. "I can't even stick to taking care of myself," she would think, adding shame to an already heavy emotional load. "Maybe I'm just meant to struggle. Maybe some of us don't get to be consistently happy."

What Keisha didn't understand was that she'd fallen into one of the most common traps of personal transformation: the "all-or-nothing" approach that sets people up for inevitable failure. In her efforts to heal completely and quickly, she'd created a routine so rigid and demanding that it couldn't survive the natural chaos and demands of adult life.

The breakthrough came when Keisha realized she'd been treating her healing practices like another work project to excel at, rather than like medicine that needed to be integrated into her actual life. She needed sustainable practices that could flex with her reality—techniques that would work whether she had five minutes or fifty, whether she was energized or exhausted, or whether life was smooth or completely overwhelming.

Keisha was about to discover that transformation doesn't happen through perfect execution of ideal practices. It happens through consistent engagement with small, flexible practices that can survive the messiness of real life and gradually reshape your internal landscape one breath, one moment, one choice at a time.

The Myth of Perfect Practice and the Reality of Sustainable Change

Many people approach personal transformation the way they were taught to approach academic or professional success: create ambitious goals, execute perfectly, and achieve dramatic results. This approach works well for external achievements but often fails miserably for internal transformation.

Why Perfectionist Approaches to Healing Fail:

Unsustainable Intensity: Elaborate routines require ideal circumstances that don't exist in real life. When life gets complicated—and it always does—these practices become impossible to maintain.

All-or-Nothing Thinking: When you can't do the "full" practice, you often abandon it entirely rather than adapting it to your current circumstances.

Shame Spiral Activation: Failed attempts at perfect practice often trigger shame, which actually reinforces the very emotional patterns you're trying to heal.

External Validation Focus: Perfectionist healing seeks to achieve an ideal state rather than build sustainable relationships with difficult emotions and experiences.

Cultural and Systemic Ignorance: Generic approaches don't account for the additional stressors that marginalized communities face, setting unrealistic expectations for what healing should look like.

For people carrying the additional burden of systemic oppression—racism, sexism, homophobia, classism—the pressure to have perfect healing practices can be especially harmful. There's often an implicit message that if you just try hard enough, meditate consistently enough, or think positively enough, you can overcome the impact of discriminatory systems through individual effort alone.

Understanding the Unique Challenges of Healing While Marginalized

Keisha's depression didn't exist in a vacuum. It was shaped by her experiences as a Black woman in spaces where she was often the only person who looked like her, where she had to work twice as hard to receive half the recognition, and where she carried the pressure of representing her entire race while never being allowed to show struggle or vulnerability.

The Additional Burden of "Strong Black Woman" Mythology: The cultural expectation that Black women should be infinitely resilient, endlessly giving, and perpetually strong creates additional pressure to hide depression and handle everything alone.

Racial Trauma and Hypervigilance: Constant exposure to microaggressions, discrimination, and systemic racism creates chronic stress that affects both mental health and the nervous system's ability to regulate.

Cultural Mistrust of Mental Health Systems: Historical and ongoing medical racism creates legitimate wariness of traditional mental health approaches that may not understand or address the impact of racial trauma.

Economic and Time Constraints: The reality of working harder for less while often supporting extended family or community creates practical barriers to elaborate self-care routines.

Intersectional Stress: The combination of racism, sexism, and other forms of discrimination creates compounding stress that generic healing approaches rarely address.

Understanding these realities is crucial for developing sustainable practices. Healing approaches that work for people with more privilege and fewer systemic stressors may not translate directly to those carrying additional burdens.

Are You Setting Yourself Up for Sustainable Success or Inevitable Failure?

As you consider Keisha's story, reflect on your own approaches to personal transformation and healing:

Signs of Unsustainable Practice Approaches:

- Creating elaborate routines that require perfect circumstances to maintain.
- Feeling like you have to do practices "completely" or not at all.
- Abandoning all practices when you can't maintain your ideal routine.
- Judging yourself harshly when you miss days or can't follow through perfectly.
- Treating healing practices like another item on your productivity to-do list.

Signs of Sustainable Integration:

- Having flexible practices that can adapt to different circumstances and energy levels.
- Focusing on consistency over perfection, showing up even when it's not ideal.
- Viewing missed days or imperfect practices as normal parts of the process.
- Approaching healing with self-compassion rather than self-judgment.
- Integrating practices into existing life rhythms rather than creating separate elaborate routines.

Additional Considerations for Marginalized Communities:

- Do your practices account for the additional stress of discrimination and systemic oppression?
- Are you trying to heal in isolation or in building community support?
- Do your practices honor your cultural background and values rather than imposing foreign approaches?

- Are you addressing both individual healing and collective/systemic factors?
- Do you have practices that work even when you're dealing with racism, sexism, or other forms of discrimination?

If you recognize patterns of perfectionist healing or approaches that don't account for your unique circumstances, you're ready to learn more sustainable ways of integrating transformation into your daily life.

Keisha's Journey: From Perfectionist Healing to Sustainable Integration

When Keisha first learned about sustainable practice approaches, she felt both relief and skepticism. Relief because it explained why her previous attempts hadn't lasted. Skepticism because she'd been conditioned to believe that anything worth doing required maximum effort and perfect execution.

Keisha started with what seemed almost embarrassingly small: three conscious breaths upon waking, one minute of body awareness during her lunch break, and thirty seconds of gratitude before sleep. *This can't possibly make a difference*, she thought. *Real healing requires more than this.*

But something unexpected began to happen. Because these practices were so manageable, Keisha could maintain them even during her most stressful weeks. When work was overwhelming, she could still practice body awareness. And when her grandmother was sick, she could still spend one minute checking in with her body. When depression made everything feel pointless, she could still find thirty seconds of gratitude, even if it was just for her morning coffee that day.

These tiny practices began to create what Keisha called "pockets of presence" throughout her day—moments when she remembered she had a choice, when she could respond rather than react, when she could offer herself the compassion she'd never learned to provide.

As these micro-practices became automatic, Keisha began expanding them gradually. Three breaths became five. One minute of body awareness became two. Thirty seconds of gratitude grew into a few minutes of reflection on meaningful moments from her day.

But the real transformation happened during a particularly difficult period when a racist incident at work triggered a depressive episode. In previous years, this would have derailed her completely—she would have abandoned all self-care practices, isolated herself, and struggled alone. This time, because her practices were so simple and sustainable, she could maintain them even while depressed.

"I realized that these small practices were like guardrails," Keisha reflected. "They didn't prevent me from struggling, but they kept me from completely losing my way. Even in my darkest moments, I had these tiny anchors that reminded me I was still here, still capable of showing up for myself."

Most importantly, Keisha began to understand her depression not as a personal failure but as a reasonable response to unreasonable circumstances. Her healing practices needed to account for the reality of navigating systemic racism while maintaining her professional success and supporting her family. This wasn't a character flaw—it was a complex challenge that required sustainable, compassionate approaches.

The Four Foundations of Sustainable Daily Integration

Based on research in habit formation, behavior change, and trauma-informed healing approaches, sustainable transformation involves four essential elements:

1. Morning Integration Practices: Starting Each Day with Embodied Awareness and Intention

How you begin your day often sets the tone for everything that follows. Morning practices don't need to be elaborate—they need to be sustainable and grounding, helping you connect with your intentions and resources before engaging with external demands.

Micro-Morning Practices (1–5 minutes):

- **Three Conscious Breaths**: Upon waking, take three slow, intentional breaths, feeling your body coming online for the day.
- **Body Check-In**: Spend thirty seconds noticing how your body feels, what it needs, and setting an intention for self-care.
- **Gratitude Moment**: Identify one thing you're genuinely grateful for, feeling the appreciation in your body rather than just thinking it.
- **Intention Setting**: Choose one word or phrase that captures how you want to show up today.

Mini-Morning Practices (5–15 minutes):

- **Embodied Morning Pages**: Write stream-of-consciousness for 5–10 minutes, letting your thoughts and feelings flow onto paper.

- **Movement Check-In**: Gentle stretching, walking, or movement that helps your body wake up and your nervous system regulate.
- **Values Reminder**: Connect with your core values and how you want to express them today.
- **Resource Activation**: Connect with your support system, spiritual practices, or sources of strength.

Flexible Morning Practices. Create 2–3 options for different circumstances:

- **High-Energy Days**: Longer practices when you have time and motivation.
- **Low-Energy Days**: Minimal practices for when depression or overwhelm is present.
- **Crisis Days**: Emergency practices for when you're barely functioning but still want to show up for yourself.

Why It Works: Morning practices create neural pathways for intentional living and help regulate your nervous system before external stressors activate old patterns.

2. Midday Reset Techniques: Maintaining Integration During Busy or Challenging Periods

The middle of the day is often when stress accumulates, old patterns get triggered, and we lose connection to our intentions and resources. Midday practices help you reset and maintain integration even during challenging periods.

Micro-Reset Practices (30 seconds to 2 minutes):

- **Breath Reset**: Take 5–10 conscious breaths to regulate your nervous system.

- **Body Scan**: Quick check-in with physical tension, posture, and what your body needs.
- **Emotional Check-In**: Notice what you're feeling and what support you might need.
- **Values Reminder**: Reconnect with how you want to show up in the next part of your day.

Bathroom Reset. Use bathroom breaks as opportunities for integration:

- Take conscious breaths while washing your hands.
- Check your posture and soften areas of tension.
- Look in the mirror and offer yourself compassion.
- Set an intention for returning to your activities.

Transition Practices. Between meetings, tasks, or activities:

- **Threshold Breaths**: Three breaths before entering new spaces or situations.
- **Completion Practices**: Acknowledge what you've accomplished before moving to the next task.
- **Energy Assessment**: Notice your energy level and what you need to sustain yourself.
- **Boundary Check**: Assess whether you're giving more than you have to give.

Cultural and Systemic Stress Navigation: Additional practices for discrimination-related stress:

- **Microaggression Recovery**: Brief practices for recovering from discriminatory interactions.
- **Code-Switching Transitions**: Practices for transitioning between different cultural contexts.
- **Safety Assessment**: Quick check-ins about physical and emotional safety in current environment.

- **Community Connection**: Brief mental connection to supportive relationships and community.

Why It Works: Midday practices prevent stress accumulation and help maintain nervous system regulation during challenging periods.

3. Evening Integration: Processing the Day's Experiences and Preparing for Restorative Rest

Evening practices help you process the day's experiences, release what doesn't serve you, and prepare your nervous system for restorative sleep. These practices are especially important for people carrying additional stress from systemic oppression.

Micro-Evening Practices (1–5 minutes):

- **Day Completion**: Acknowledge one thing you accomplished and one challenge you navigated.
- **Emotional Release**: Brief practice for releasing stress, frustration, or accumulated tension.
- **Gratitude Practice**: Identify 1–3 things you're grateful for from the day.
- **Tomorrow's Intention**: Set a gentle intention for how you want to approach tomorrow.

Processing Practices (5–15 minutes):

- **Journaling**: Write about your day's experiences, focusing on emotions and insights rather than just events.
- **Body-Based Release**: Gentle movement, stretching, or somatic practices to release the day's tension.
- **Emotional Integration**: Process difficult emotions from the day using techniques from previous weeks.

- **Relationship Review**: Reflect on your interactions and what they revealed about your patterns.

Preparation for Rest:

- **Nervous System Settling**: Practices that activate your parasympathetic nervous system for sleep.
- **Worry Time**: Designated time to acknowledge concerns rather than carrying them into sleep.
- **Safe Space Creation**: Physical and energetic practices for creating safety for rest.
- **Future Self Connection**: Brief visualization of waking up refreshed and resourced.

Racial Trauma Processing: Additional practices for people experiencing discrimination:

- **Discrimination Discharge**: Specific practices for releasing the impact of racist interactions.
- **Cultural Affirmation**: Connection to cultural strengths, community, and positive identity.
- **Systemic Perspective**: Practices that separate personal worth from systemic oppression.
- **Ancestor/Community Connection**: Drawing strength from cultural heritage and community resilience.

Why It Works: Evening practices help prevent stress accumulation, process difficult experiences, and prepare your nervous system for restorative sleep.

4. Crisis Navigation: Tools for Maintaining Integration During Particularly Difficult Periods

Life inevitably includes periods of crisis, trauma, illness, loss, or overwhelming stress. Having practices specifically designed for these times helps maintain some level of integration even when you can barely function.

Emergency Self-Care Practices (30 seconds to 2 minutes):

- **Crisis Breathing**: Simple breathing techniques that work even during panic or overwhelm.
- **Grounding Touch**: Physical practices for staying connected to your body during dissociation or overwhelm.
- **Safety Mantras**: Brief phrases that remind you of your resilience and support system.
- **Minimum Viable Self-Care**: The absolute smallest acts of self-care you can manage.

Adaptation Strategies:

- **Scaling Down**: How to adapt your regular practices when you have less energy or capacity.
- **Support Activation**: Quick ways to access your support system during difficult times.
- **Professional Resources**: When to seek additional help and how to access it.
- **Crisis Prevention**: Early warning signs and intervention strategies.

Systemic Crisis Navigation: Additional considerations for discrimination-related crises:

- **Racial Trauma First Aid**: Immediate practices for acute discrimination experiences.
- **Community Support**: How to access culturally competent support during a crisis.
- **Safety Planning**: Practical and emotional safety strategies for hostile environments.

- **Systemic Perspective**: Maintaining awareness that individual crises may reflect systemic problems.

Recovery and Integration:

- **Post-Crisis Processing**: How to process and integrate difficult experiences.
- **Gradual Re-Engagement**: Slowly returning to regular practices after crisis periods.
- **Learning Integration**: Identifying what the crisis taught you about your needs and resources.
- **Resilience Building**: Using crisis experiences to build greater capacity for future challenges.

Why It Works: Crisis navigation tools prevent complete derailment during difficult periods and help maintain connection to resources and support even when overwhelmed.

Applying Sustainable Integration to Keisha's Life

As Keisha developed these sustainable daily practices, her relationship with both her healing journey and her depression transformed completely. Instead of elaborate routines that required perfect circumstances, she had flexible practices that could adapt to her real life as a Black woman navigating corporate America while dealing with mental health challenges.

Her morning practice became three conscious breaths and one intention word, taking less than thirty seconds but providing a foundation for intentional living. During particularly stressful workdays, she'd use bathroom breaks for micro-resets—breathing, checking her posture, and offering herself compassion.

Evenings became sacred time for processing not just personal stress but the additional burden of workplace discrimination. Keisha developed practices specifically for "discharging racism"—brief somatic techniques for releasing the impact of microaggressions and reconnecting with her cultural strength and community support.

Most importantly, Keisha learned to approach depression as a visitor rather than an enemy. When depressive episodes arose, instead of abandoning all self-care, she would scale her practices to match her capacity. On days when she could barely get out of bed, she might just take three breaths and acknowledge that she was struggling. On better days, she could expand her practices to include journaling, movement, or community connection.

"I realized that consistency mattered more than intensity," Keisha reflected. "My tiny daily practices created more transformation than my elaborate weekend retreats ever did. And when I stopped trying to heal myself out of being Black in America and started developing practices that honored both my struggles and my strength, everything shifted."

The Neuroscience of Sustainable Change: Small Practices, Big Results

Research in neuroscience confirms what Keisha discovered through experience: small, consistent practices create more lasting change than intense, inconsistent efforts. This happens because:

Neuroplasticity Responds to Repetition: Your brain changes through repeated experience, not through intensity. Daily micro-practices create stronger neural pathways than occasional elaborate practices.

Habit Formation Requires Consistency: New habits form through consistent repetition in similar contexts, not through perfect execution of ideal behaviors.

Stress Response Patterns: Sustainable practices work with your nervous system's natural rhythms rather than fighting against them, creating less resistance and more integration.

Identity Integration: Small daily practices gradually shift your sense of identity from "someone who struggles with depression" to "someone who consistently shows up for themselves."

Cultural Competence: Practices that honor your cultural background and account for systemic stressors are more likely to be sustainable because they work with your reality rather than against it.

Building Your Personalized Daily Integration System

Creating sustainable daily practices requires honoring both your healing needs and your real-life circumstances. The goal is consistency over perfection, creating gentle habits that can survive the messiness of actual life.

Start Embarrassingly Small: Choose practices so small they feel almost silly—three breaths, one grateful thought, thirty seconds of body awareness. You can always expand, but you need to establish consistency first.

Create Multiple Options: Develop 2–3 versions of each practice for different energy levels and circumstances. High-energy days, low-energy days, and crisis days all need different approaches.

Honor Your Cultural Context: Make sure your practices align with your cultural values and account for any additional stressors you face due to discrimination or systemic oppression.

Build on Existing Habits: Attach new practices to habits you already have rather than creating entirely new routines. Breathe while brushing your teeth, check in with your body while commuting, and practice gratitude while preparing meals.

Track Consistency, Not Perfection: Measure success by how many days you show up, not by how perfectly you execute ideal practices.

Your Week 7 Action Plan: The Sustainable Integration Implementation Guide

This week focuses on creating daily practices that can survive real life while gradually transforming your internal landscape. You'll develop morning, midday, and evening practices that are sustainable, flexible, and culturally responsive to your unique circumstances.

Day 1–2: Morning Integration Development

Current Morning Routine Assessment. Examine your current morning patterns:

- How do you typically start your day emotionally and physically?
- What time constraints and energy levels do you usually have in the morning?
- What cultural or family responsibilities shape your morning routine?
- What currently works well in your mornings, and what creates stress?

Micro-Morning Practice Design. Create three versions of morning practices (1–5 minutes each):

Version 1: High Energy/Extra Time

- 5–10 conscious breaths with intention setting.
- 2–3 minutes of gentle movement or stretching.
- Brief gratitude practice with embodied appreciation.
- Values connection and daily intention setting.

Version 2: Normal Energy/Limited Time

- Three conscious breaths upon waking.
- Thirty-second body check-in.
- One gratitude acknowledgment.
- Single intention word for the day.

Version 3: Low Energy/Crisis Mode

- Three breaths while still in bed.
- Brief self-compassion phrase ("I'm doing the best I can").
- Acknowledge that showing up at all is enough.

Implementation Practice: Try each version on different days, noticing which feels most sustainable for your typical circumstances.

Cultural Integration. Consider how to honor your cultural background in morning practices:

- Prayer or spiritual practices from your tradition.
- Connection to ancestors or community strength.
- Affirmations that honor your identity and resilience.
- Practices that prepare you for potential discrimination or cultural navigation.

Key Goal: Establish morning practices so simple and flexible they can be maintained regardless of circumstances.

Day 3–4: Midday Reset and Crisis Navigation

Daily Stress Pattern Recognition. Track your typical daily stress accumulation:

- What times of day do you typically feel most activated or overwhelmed?
- What specific situations trigger your depression, anxiety, or anger patterns?
- How do discrimination or systemic stresses show up in your daily life?
- What early warning signs indicate you need to reset or seek support?

Micro-Reset Practice Development. Create brief practices for different midday scenarios:

Bathroom Reset (30 seconds to 1 minute):

- Five conscious breaths while washing hands.
- Quick posture check and tension release.
- Brief self-compassion phrase or affirmation.
- Intention setting for returning to activities.

Meeting/Task Transition (15–30 seconds):

- Three breaths before entering new situations.
- Quick energy and capacity assessment.
- Boundary check ("Am I giving more than I have?").
- Values reminder of how you want to show up.

Discrimination Recovery (1–2 minutes for racial/cultural stress):

- Breathing practice to discharge activation from microaggressions.
- Brief connection to cultural strength and community support.
- Reminder that individual worth isn't determined by systemic oppression.
- Quick safety assessment of the current environment.

Crisis Navigation Tools. Develop emergency practices for overwhelming moments:

- **Crisis Breathing**: Simple breath techniques that work during panic.
- **Grounding Touch**: Physical contact with solid surfaces or self-holding.
- **Safety Phrases**: Brief mantras that remind you of your resilience.
- **Support Access**: Quick ways to reach out for help when needed.

Key Goal: Create sustainable midday practices that prevent stress accumulation and provide tools for crisis moments.

Day 5–6: Evening Integration and Processing

Evening Routine Assessment. Evaluate your current evening patterns:

- How do you typically end your workday and transition to personal time?
- What helps or hinders your ability to process daily experiences?

- How do you currently handle accumulated stress from discrimination or difficult interactions?
- What supports or interferes with your preparation for restorative sleep?

Evening Integration Practice Design. Create flexible evening practices for processing and preparation:

Micro-Evening Practice (2–5 minutes):

- **Day Completion**: Acknowledge one accomplishment and one challenge navigated.
- **Emotional Check-In**: Notice what you're carrying and what needs attention.
- **Gratitude Practice**: Identify 1–3 genuine appreciations from the day.
- **Tomorrow's Gentle Intention**: Set a compassionate intention for tomorrow.

Extended Evening Practice (10–20 minutes when you have the capacity):

- Stream-of-consciousness journaling about the day's experiences.
- Body-based tension release through gentle movement or somatic practices.
- Discrimination processing if you experienced racism, sexism, or other systemic stress.
- Community connection through prayer, meditation, or mental connection to support system.

Sleep Preparation Practices:

- **Worry Time**: 2–3 minutes to acknowledge concerns rather than carrying them to bed.

- **Nervous System Settling**: Breathing or movement practices that activate rest response.
- **Safe Space Creation**: Physical and energetic practices for creating safety for sleep.
- **Cultural Affirmation**: Connection to cultural strengths and positive identity before rest.

Racial Trauma Evening Processing: Additional practices for discrimination-related stress

- **Discharge Practices**: Somatic techniques for releasing racism's physical impact.
- **Cultural Strength Connection**: Practices that connect you to community resilience and heritage.
- **Systemic Perspective**: Separating personal worth from systemic oppression.
- **Ancestor Strength**: Drawing on cultural and familial resilience traditions.

Key Goal: Develop evening practices that process daily experiences and prepare your nervous system for restorative rest.

Day 7: Integration and Sustainable System Creation

Weekly Practice Review. Assess your week's experiments with sustainable practices:

- Which practices felt most natural and sustainable?
- What helped you maintain consistency even during challenging days?
- How did cultural integration support or challenge your practices?
- What modifications would make your practices more sustainable?

Personal Integration System Design: Create your customized daily practice system

Morning Options (choose based on daily capacity):

- High-energy version for days when you have time and motivation.
- Standard version for typical circumstances.
- Low-energy version for difficult days or crisis periods.

Midday Options (available throughout the day):

- Micro-resets for busy periods.
- Transition practices between activities.
- Crisis navigation tools for overwhelming moments.
- Discrimination recovery practices as needed.

Evening Options (flexible based on energy and circumstances):

- Brief completion and gratitude practices.
- Extended processing when you have capacity.
- Cultural affirmation and community connection.
- Sleep preparation and nervous system settling.

Crisis Protocol: Emergency practices for particularly difficult periods:

- Minimum viable self-care (what you can do when barely functioning).
- Support activation strategies (how to reach out for help).
- Adaptation approaches (scaling practices to match capacity).
- Recovery and re-engagement (how to gradually return to regular practices).

Cultural Integration: Ensure your practices honor your background and circumstances:

- How do your practices connect to your cultural strengths and heritage?
- Do they account for additional stresses from discrimination or systemic oppression?
- Are they sustainable within your family and community context?
- Do they support both individual healing and collective resilience?

Sustainability Assessment. Evaluate your system for long-term maintenance:

- Are these practices small enough to maintain during busy periods?
- Do you have options for different energy levels and circumstances?
- Can you maintain consistency even when not feeling motivated?
- Do they work with your real life rather than requiring ideal circumstances?

Weekly Success Metrics

By the end of Week 7, you should be able to:

- Maintain morning practices regardless of energy level or time constraints.
- Use midday reset techniques to prevent stress accumulation.
- Process daily experiences through sustainable evening practices.

- Access crisis navigation tools during overwhelming periods.
- Adapt all practices to honor your cultural background and account for systemic stressors.

Troubleshooting Common Challenges

"I keep forgetting to do the practices." Start smaller. If you're forgetting three breaths, try one breath. Attach practices to existing habits rather than creating new routines.

"The practices feel too simple to make a difference." Small, consistent practices create more neural change than intense, sporadic efforts. Trust the process and focus on consistency over intensity.

"I feel guilty that I can't do 'more' for my healing." This perfectionist mindset actually interferes with healing. Sustainable practices that honor your real life are more effective than ideal practices you can't maintain.

"My cultural/family context doesn't support these practices." Adapt practices to fit your context rather than fighting against it. Find ways to integrate healing into existing cultural or family patterns.

"I abandon everything when I'm depressed/overwhelmed." This is exactly when micro-practices are most valuable. Having crisis-level practices prevents complete abandonment of self-care during difficult periods.

Guided Sustainable Integration Session: Creating Your Daily Practice Foundation

Allow approximately 20–25 minutes for this integration and planning session. This practice focuses on connecting with sustainable approaches to daily healing and transformation.

Find a comfortable position that feels both supported and alert. Since this practice involves planning your sustainable healing approach, choose a space where you feel emotionally safe and can think clearly about your real-life circumstances and needs.

Take a moment to acknowledge the wisdom of seeking sustainable rather than perfect approaches to healing. In a culture that often demands immediate results and flawless execution, choosing gentle consistency over dramatic transformation is an act of self-compassion and practical wisdom.

Begin with several natural breaths, feeling your body's natural rhythm of expansion and release. Notice that your breath doesn't try to be perfect—it simply continues, moment by moment, sustaining your life through consistent, gentle repetition. This is the model for sustainable healing practices.

Let's start by connecting with your current reality rather than an idealized version of how you think your life should be. Bring to awareness your typical day—your energy levels, time constraints, responsibilities, and challenges. Include both the universal human challenges and any additional stressors you face due to discrimination, cultural navigation, or systemic oppression.

Instead of judging these realities as obstacles to healing, practice seeing them as the context within which your healing must occur. Your practices need to work with your actual life, not against it.

Now let's connect with what sustainable practice feels like in your body. Think of something you do consistently without much effort—brushing your teeth, making coffee, or checking your phone. Notice that these activities don't require motivation or perfect circumstances. They've become integrated into your life through repetition and practicality.

Feel what it would be like to approach healing practices with this same naturalness—not as additional burdens or tests of your worthiness, but as simple acts of self-care woven into the fabric of your daily life.

Let's explore what your authentic morning needs might be. Instead of thinking about ideal morning routines, notice what your body and nervous system actually need when you first wake up. Do you need gentle activation or calming regulation? Do you need connection to your values or simply acknowledgment of your current state?

Imagine a morning practice so simple and natural that you could do it even on your most challenging days. Maybe it's three conscious breaths while still in bed. Maybe it's placing your hand on your heart and acknowledging that you're doing your best. Maybe it's a brief connection to something or someone you're grateful for or something or someone that gives your life meaning.

Feel how different this is from forcing yourself through elaborate routines that require perfect circumstances and high motivation.

Now let's consider your midday reality. Bring to awareness the typical stresses, demands, and challenges you encounter during your day. If you face discrimination or systemic oppression, acknowledge these additional burdens with compassion rather than trying to minimize or ignore them.

Instead of seeing these challenges as problems to solve, consider them as signals for when you need brief moments of reset and self-care. Imagine having micro-practices available throughout your day—tiny moments of breathing, body awareness, or self-compassion that can help you maintain your center even during difficult circumstances.

Visualize yourself using bathroom breaks for brief resets, taking conscious breaths before entering challenging situations, or offering yourself internal compassion after difficult interactions. These aren't elaborate practices—they're simply moments of returning to yourself throughout the day.

Let's explore what sustainable evening integration might look like for you. Consider how you typically end your days and what helps you transition from external demands to rest and restoration. If you carry additional stress from navigating discrimination or cultural challenges, acknowledge that your evening processing needs might be different from others.

Imagine evening practices that help you discharge the day's accumulated stress, process any difficult experiences, and prepare your nervous system for restorative sleep. These might include brief journaling, gentle movement, gratitude practices, or cultural affirmations that reconnect you to your strength and community.

Most importantly, imagine approaching your evening not as another series of tasks to complete perfectly, but as sacred time for releasing what doesn't serve you and preparing for rest.

Now let's create your crisis navigation plan. Bring to awareness the times when you're most likely to abandon all self-care—during depression, overwhelm, illness, or particular stress.

Instead of judging these times as failures, see them as exactly the times when you most need gentle, accessible practices.

Imagine having practices so simple that you could maintain them even when barely functioning. Maybe it's just one conscious breath. Maybe it's placing your hand on your heart and acknowledging your struggle. Maybe it's a brief mental connection to one person who cares about you.

Feel how having these emergency practices could serve as guardrails, preventing complete disconnection from self-care even during your most challenging periods.

Let's integrate your cultural identity and community strength into your practices. Consider how your cultural background, family traditions, or community connections could support rather than compete with your healing practices.

Maybe your practices include prayer or spiritual elements from your tradition. Maybe they involve mental connection to ancestors or community resilience. Maybe they incorporate cultural affirmations that honor both your struggles and your strength.

Imagine practices that don't ask you to abandon your cultural identity but rather draw strength from it, creating healing approaches that honor both your individual needs and your community context.

Now let's set realistic intentions for your sustainable practice system. Instead of committing to dramatic changes, focus on small, manageable shifts that you can realistically maintain.

Choose one simple morning practice.

Chapter 11

Week 8: Embodied Resilience—Thriving Through Life's Challenges

The Storm That Taught Resilience

At 46, Elena thought she had finally figured out life. After years of struggling with anxiety that would spike without warning and anger that seemed to consume her from the inside, she had developed a solid routine of somatic practices, emotional integration skills, and daily rhythms that kept her centered. As a single mother working as a nurse, she'd learned to navigate the constant demands on her time and energy while maintaining her emotional equilibrium.

Then life delivered what felt like a perfect storm. Within six weeks, Elena's teenage daughter was diagnosed with a chronic illness requiring frequent medical appointments and lifestyle changes. Her elderly mother fell and needed temporary care. The hospital where she worked underwent massive layoffs, leaving her with double the patient load and constant job insecurity. Her car broke down, requiring expensive repairs she couldn't afford. Her ex-husband, who had been mostly absent from their daughter's life, suddenly reappeared demanding changes to custody arrangements.

Elena's first thought was, "All my healing work is useless. I'm right back where I started." The familiar anxiety symptoms returned—racing heart, tight chest, spiraling thoughts about everything that could go wrong. Anger flared at the unfairness of it all, at her ex-husband's timing, and at a healthcare system that prioritized profits over patients and workers. Moments of depression crept in when the weight of it all felt impossible to bear.

But something was different this time. Instead of being completely derailed by these challenges, Elena found herself responding from a deeper place of strength she didn't know she possessed. Yes, she felt anxious—but she could feel the anxiety in her body and breathe with it instead of being consumed by it. Yes, she felt angry—but she could channel that energy into advocating for her daughter's needs and setting clear boundaries with her ex-husband instead of exploding or imploding.

Most remarkably, Elena discovered that her seven weeks of integration work had created what she called "emotional muscle memory." Even when her conscious mind was overwhelmed, her body remembered how to find its center. Her nervous system had learned new patterns of regulation that didn't disappear under pressure—they actually became more available when she needed them most.

"I realized that resilience isn't about not having problems," Elena reflected months later. "It's about having a relationship with problems that don't destroy you. My anxiety, anger, and depression didn't disappear during that crisis—they became tools for navigating it. The anxiety kept me alert to what needed attention. The anger gave me energy to fight for what mattered. Even the depression forced me to slow down and prioritize what was truly essential."

Elena was discovering what researchers call "embodied resilience"—the capacity to navigate life's inevitable difficulties while maintaining connection to your body's wisdom, your emotional intelligence, your relational capacity, and your sense of meaning. This wasn't just surviving challenges—it was growing stronger and more integrated through them.

Understanding True Resilience: Beyond Just "Bouncing Back"

Traditional concepts of resilience often focus on "bouncing back" to a previous state after adversity. But this understanding misses something crucial: **true resilience isn't about returning to where you were—it's about integrating challenges in ways that expand your capacity for wisdom, compassion, and authentic living.**

Mechanical Resilience (bouncing back). Returning to previous functioning after adversity, often through suppression, avoidance, or sheer willpower. This approach may work short-term but often leads to:

- Accumulated stress that eventually overwhelms the system.
- Repeated patterns because underlying issues aren't addressed.
- Emotional numbing or disconnection as coping mechanisms.

- Burnout from constantly trying to maintain an unsustainable pace.

Embodied Resilience (growing through). Using challenges as opportunities for deeper integration, expanded capacity, and more authentic living. This includes:

- **Somatic Resilience**: Your body's ability to move through activation and return to regulation while building greater capacity for future challenges.
- **Emotional Resilience**: The skill to feel difficult emotions fully without being overwhelmed, using them as information and fuel for authentic action.
- **Relational Resilience**: The capacity to maintain authentic connections during stress and to seek appropriate support when needed.
- **Meaning-Making Resilience**: The ability to find purpose and growth opportunities even within difficult experiences.
- **Integrative Resilience**: The capacity to hold multiple perspectives simultaneously—feeling difficult emotions while maintaining hope, acknowledging problems while staying connected to resources.

The Neuroscience of Integrated Resilience

Research in neuroscience and trauma recovery shows that embodied resilience creates measurable changes in brain structure and function:

Enhanced Prefrontal Cortex Function: Better executive functioning, emotional regulation, and decision-making under stress. This allows you to respond rather than react during challenges.

Improved Vagal Tone: Stronger parasympathetic nervous system response, leading to better stress recovery and social engagement capacity. You can calm down more quickly after activation and stay connected to others during difficulties.

Increased Neuroplasticity: Greater ability to form new neural pathways and recover from traumatic experiences. Your brain becomes more flexible and adaptive.

Integrated Default Mode Network: More coherent sense of self that persists even during challenging periods. You maintain connection to your values and identity even under stress.

Strengthened Insula Function: Better interoceptive awareness (body sensation recognition) that supports emotional regulation and decision-making. You can use body wisdom to guide choices during difficult times.

These neurological changes explain why Elena could access her integration skills even during a crisis—her brain had literally rewired to support embodied resilience rather than just crisis survival.

Are You Building Mechanical or Embodied Resilience?

As you consider Elena's experience, reflect on your own patterns of navigating life's challenges:

Signs of Mechanical Resilience (less sustainable):

- Pushing through difficulties without processing their emotional impact.
- "Bouncing back" quickly but finding similar problems recurring.
- Using willpower, suppression, or avoidance as primary coping strategies.

- Feeling proud of how much you can handle without support.
- Treating emotions as obstacles to overcome rather than information to integrate.
- Maintaining the same patterns that created problems in the first place.

Signs of Embodied Resilience (more sustainable):

- Moving through challenges while staying connected to your body's wisdom.
- Using difficult experiences as opportunities for growth and deeper self-knowledge.
- Feeling emotions fully while maintaining the capacity for wise action.
- Seeking appropriate support and maintaining relationships during stress.
- Finding meaning and purpose even within difficult circumstances.
- Integrating lessons from challenges to create more authentic, sustainable patterns.

Trauma-Informed Resilience: For people with trauma histories, embodied resilience includes:

- Recognizing trauma responses without being overwhelmed by them.
- Having tools for regulation that work even during triggering circumstances.
- Distinguishing between past trauma and present challenges.
- Building capacity gradually rather than forcing healing.
- Honoring protective responses while creating new options

If you recognize patterns of mechanical resilience, you're ready to develop more sustainable, embodied approaches to life's inevitable challenges.

Elena's Journey: From Surviving to Thriving Through Crisis

When Elena first encountered her perfect storm, her initial reaction was familiar—panic, overwhelm, and the belief that her healing work had failed. But as she began to apply the integration skills she'd developed over the previous seven weeks, something remarkable happened.

Instead of abandoning her practices during a crisis, Elena adapted them. Her morning breathing practice became an anchor that she could access even when waking up anxious about the day's challenges. Her midday resets became essential tools for maintaining sanity during twelve-hour shifts at the hospital. Her evening integration practices helped her process not just her own stress but also support her daughter through medical appointments and treatment decisions.

Most importantly, Elena learned to recognize her early warning signs before they became overwhelming. She noticed that her shoulders would tense and her breathing would become shallow before anxiety spiraled. She observed that her jaw would clench and her hands would form fists before anger exploded. She recognized that her chest would feel heavy and her energy would drop before depression settled in.

With these early warning signs, Elena could intervene before patterns became overwhelming. A few conscious breaths when she noticed shoulder tension could prevent a full anxiety attack. Acknowledging her anger and asking what boundary needed protection could prevent explosive conflicts with her ex-husband. Recognizing early signs of depression and reaching out for support could prevent complete withdrawal and isolation.

Elena's support network became crucial during this period. Instead of trying to handle everything alone, she learned to ask for specific help: childcare during her mother's medical appointments, meal support during her daughter's treatment, and emotional support from friends who understood her situation. She realized that seeking support wasn't weakness—it was wisdom.

Most profoundly, Elena discovered that the crisis was revealing strengths and capacities she hadn't known she possessed. Her nursing skills became invaluable in advocating for her daughter's medical care. Her experience with difficult emotions helped her support her daughter through diagnosis and treatment fears. Her hard-won boundary skills helped her navigate co-parenting challenges with her ex-husband.

"I realized that everything I'd learned wasn't just for the good times," Elena reflected. "It was preparation for the hard times. My body remembered how to find its center even when my mind was spinning. My emotions became allies instead of enemies. Even my depression became a teacher, showing me what I needed to let go of and what truly mattered."

The Four Pillars of Embodied Resilience

Based on research in post-traumatic growth, resilience psychology, and somatic therapy, embodied resilience involves four essential capacities:

1. Early Warning Systems: Recognizing When Old Patterns Are Trying to Reassert Themselves

Embodied resilience begins with the ability to recognize when you're moving toward dysregulation before it becomes overwhelming. This requires developing sophisticated awareness of your unique early warning signs and triggers.

Somatic Early Warning Signs. Learn to recognize the physical precursors to emotional overwhelm:

- **Anxiety Signals**: Subtle changes in breathing, muscle tension, or heart rate that precede anxiety spirals.
- **Depression Indicators**: Early signs of energy depletion, postural collapse, or withdrawal impulses.
- **Anger Precursors**: Initial muscle tension, heat, or activation that occurs before anger becomes overwhelming.
- **Trauma Activation**: Physical signs that past trauma is being triggered by current circumstances.

Emotional Pattern Recognition. Develop awareness of thought and feeling patterns that indicate you're moving toward old coping strategies:

- Catastrophic thinking patterns that spiral toward anxiety.
- Self-critical thoughts that reinforce depressive episodes.
- Blame or victimization thinking that fuels destructive anger.
- Dissociation or numbing impulses that indicate overwhelm.

Situational Triggers. Identify the circumstances, relationships, or environments that most consistently activate old patterns:

- Specific interpersonal dynamics that trigger your attachment wounds.
- Work or family stressors that overwhelm your nervous system.
- Anniversary dates or seasonal patterns that affect your emotional state.
- Social or cultural situations that activate trauma or identity stress.

Intervention Timing. Learn to intervene at the optimal moment for effectiveness:

- **Green Zone**: Calm, regulated state where prevention practices are most effective.
- **Yellow Zone**: Early activation where intervention can prevent escalation.
- **Red Zone**: High activation where crisis management tools are needed.
- **Recovery Zone**: Post-crisis period where integration and learning can occur.

Why It Works: Early intervention is far more effective than crisis management. When you can catch patterns as they're emerging, you have more options for response and less neurological momentum to overcome.

2. Intervention Strategies: Effective Tools for Redirecting Dysregulation Before It Becomes Overwhelming

Having awareness of early warning signs is only valuable if you have effective tools for intervention. Embodied resilience requires a tool kit of practices that can shift nervous system states quickly and effectively.

Somatic Intervention Techniques:

- **Breath Regulation:** Specific breathing patterns that calm anxiety, energize depression, or discharge anger.
- **Progressive Muscle Relaxation:** Systematic tension and release to reset nervous system activation.
- **Grounding Practices:** Techniques that use physical sensation to anchor you in present-moment reality.
- **Movement Interventions:** Specific movements that help discharge activation or restore regulation.

Cognitive-Somatic Integration:

- **Thought-Body Tracking:** Noticing how different thoughts create physical sensations and using this awareness to shift both.
- **Reframing from Resources:** Challenging distorted thinking from a regulated nervous system state rather than while activated.
- **Values-Based Decision-Making:** Using your core values to guide choices during emotional intensity.
- **Perspective-Taking:** Practices that help you see situations from multiple viewpoints.

Emotional Alchemy. Transforming difficult emotions into fuel for positive action:

- **Anxiety → Preparation:** Using anxious energy for thorough planning and preparation.
- **Depression → Reflection:** Using depressive introspection for life evaluation and meaningful change.
- **Anger → Boundaries:** Using angry energy for protection and authentic self-advocacy.

- **Fear → Caution**: Using fear as information about what needs attention or protection.

Relational Interventions. Using relationships as resources for regulation:

- **Co-Regulation Seeking**: Knowing when and how to seek support from others.
- **Communication Skills**: Expressing your needs clearly during emotional intensity.
- **Boundary Setting**: Protecting your energy and capacity during challenging periods.
- **Conflict Navigation**: Tools for maintaining connection during disagreement or stress.

Why It Works: Having multiple intervention strategies gives you options for different situations and prevents you from feeling helpless when old patterns emerge.

3. Support Network Development: Creating Relationships That Support Your Ongoing Integration

Embodied resilience cannot be sustained in isolation. Human nervous systems are designed to regulate through connection with other regulated systems. Building and maintaining supportive relationships is essential for long-term emotional integration.

Support Network Assessment. Evaluate your current relationships:

- **Regulation Supporters**: People whose presence helps you feel calm and centered.
- **Growth Partners**: Relationships that support your ongoing development and authenticity.

- **Crisis Resources**: People you can turn to during particularly difficult periods.
- **Professional Support**: Therapists, coaches, or other professionals who understand your journey.

Reciprocal Support. Develop relationships based on mutual support rather than one-way dependence:

- **Giving and Receiving**: Learning to both offer and accept support comfortably.
- **Emotional Reciprocity**: Relationships where both people can be authentic about struggles and growth.
- **Boundary Respect**: Connections that honor both people's limits and capacity.
- **Growth Encouragement**: Relationships that support each other's ongoing development.

Community Building. Connect with larger communities that share your values and support your growth:

- **Interest-Based Communities**: Groups organized around activities or causes you care about.
- **Identity Communities**: Connections with people who share important aspects of your identity.
- **Healing Communities**: Support groups, therapy groups, or other healing-focused connections.
- **Service Communities**: Groups focused on contributing to causes larger than individual concerns.

Professional Support Systems. Maintain connections with professionals who understand embodied approaches to healing:

- **Trauma-Informed Therapists**: Professionals who understand the integration of mind and body in healing.

- **Somatic Practitioners**: Bodyworkers, movement therapists, or others who work with nervous system regulation.
- **Medical Support**: Healthcare providers who understand the mind-body connection in health.
- **Spiritual Support**: Religious or spiritual leaders who support your meaning-making and purpose.

Why It Works: Supportive relationships provide both co-regulation in crisis and ongoing encouragement for continued growth. They normalize the challenges of emotional integration and provide perspective during difficult periods.

4. Continuous Growth Planning: Setting Intentions for Deepening Transformation Beyond the Eight Weeks

Embodied resilience includes the understanding that emotional integration is not a destination but an ongoing journey of deepening awareness, capacity, and authenticity. Planning for continued growth prevents stagnation and provides direction for ongoing development.

Integration Deepening. Identify areas where you want to continue developing:

- **Somatic Awareness**: Continuing to refine your ability to read and respond to body signals.
- **Emotional Intelligence**: Developing more nuanced understanding of emotional messages and responses.
- **Relational Skills**: Growing in your capacity for authentic, boundaried connection.
- **Meaning-Making**: Continuing to align your life with your deepest values and purpose.

Skill Development Planning. Create specific plans for ongoing skill development:

- **Advanced Practices**: More sophisticated somatic, emotional, or relational practices.
- **Learning Opportunities**: Workshops, classes, or trainings that support your continued growth.
- **Reading and Study**: Books, articles, or other resources that deepen your understanding.
- **Practice Groups**: Communities focused on ongoing practice and development.

Life Integration. Plan for how to integrate your learning into major life areas:

- **Work Integration**: Bringing embodied awareness and emotional intelligence to professional life.
- **Relationship Integration**: Applying your learning to family, friendship, and romantic relationships.
- **Parenting Integration**: Using embodied approaches in raising children (if applicable).
- **Community Integration**: Contributing your skills and insights to your broader community.

Challenge Preparation. Anticipate future challenges and prepare responses:

- **Predictable Stressors**: Seasonal, anniversary, or life-stage challenges you can anticipate.
- **Growth Edges**: Areas where you expect continued challenges as you grow.
- **Support Needs**: What additional support you might need for future challenges.

- **Skill Gaps**: Areas where you want to develop additional capacity.

Legacy Planning. Consider how your healing contributes to larger healing:

- **Generational Healing**: How your integration affects family patterns and future generations.
- **Community Contribution**: Ways your healing can contribute to collective healing.
- **Mentorship**: Opportunities to support others on similar journeys.
- **Social Impact**: How your embodied resilience can contribute to positive social change.

Why It Works: Continuous growth planning maintains momentum and direction while preventing the stagnation that can occur when people feel they've "completed" their healing work.

Applying Embodied Resilience to Elena's Ongoing Journey

As Elena integrated these four pillars of embodied resilience, her entire relationship with life's challenges transformed. The crisis that had initially felt like proof of her healing failure became evidence of how much she had actually grown.

Elena's early warning system became so sophisticated that she could often catch patterns before they fully activated. She noticed that certain family dynamics would trigger her people-pleasing patterns, that work stress would activate her hypervigilance, and that her daughter's medical appointments would sometimes trigger her own medical trauma from childhood.

Her intervention tool kit expanded to include practices specifically designed for the challenges she faced as a single mother in healthcare. She developed breathing techniques that worked during twelve-hour shifts, boundary practices for dealing with difficult family members, and energy management strategies for balancing caregiving responsibilities.

Most importantly, Elena's support network became a crucial foundation for her resilience. She joined a support group for parents of children with chronic illnesses, maintained a regular connection with a therapist who understood somatic approaches, and cultivated friendships with other single mothers who shared similar challenges.

Elena's continuous growth planning included returning to school for a degree in holistic health, with the goal of eventually opening a practice that integrated conventional nursing with somatic and emotional healing approaches. Her personal healing had become a foundation for contributing to collective healing.

"I realized that resilience isn't about becoming invulnerable," Elena reflected. "It's about becoming more fully human—more able to feel everything life brings while staying connected to what matters most. My struggles became my strengths, my wounds became my wisdom, and my healing became a gift I could offer to others."

The Lifelong Journey of Embodied Emotional Intelligence

As you complete this 8-week protocol, it's important to understand that you're not graduating from emotional work—you're beginning a lifelong journey of deepening integration and embodied wisdom. The skills you've developed are not final achievements but foundational capacities that will continue to evolve and deepen throughout your life.

Emotional Mastery vs. Emotional Fluency: The goal isn't to master emotions by controlling them but to develop fluency—the ability to work skillfully with whatever emotions arise, using them as information and energy for authentic living.

Healing vs. Growing: While healing involves recovering from past wounds, growing involves continuously expanding your capacity for wisdom, love, and authentic expression. Both are ongoing processes.

Individual vs. Collective: Your personal healing contributes to collective healing. As you develop embodied resilience, you become a resource for others and contribute to positive social change.

Integration vs. Perfection: The goal isn't to achieve perfect emotional regulation but to develop increasingly sophisticated skills for working with the full spectrum of human experience.

Building Your Embodied Resilience System

Developing embodied resilience requires ongoing attention to all four pillars while maintaining the integration practices you've developed over the previous seven weeks.

Daily Resilience Practices: Maintain the foundation practices that support ongoing integration while adding resilience-specific elements:

- Morning practices that include early warning sign awareness.
- Midday practices that include intervention skill rehearsal.

- Evening practices that include support network appreciation and continuous growth planning.

Weekly Resilience Review. Regularly assess your resilience development:

- What challenges did you navigate this week, and how did you handle them?
- Which early warning signs are you getting better at recognizing?
- What intervention strategies were most effective?
- How did your support network contribute to your resilience?
- What areas of growth are calling for attention?

Monthly Resilience Planning. Use your growing awareness to plan for continued development:

- What predictable challenges are approaching, and how can you prepare?
- Which resilience skills need strengthening?
- How can you deepen your support network?
- What opportunities for growth and contribution are emerging?

Annual Resilience Assessment: Take time each year to evaluate your overall resilience development and set intentions for continued growth.

Your Week 8 Action Plan: The Embodied Resilience Implementation Guide

This final week integrates everything you've learned while building specific capacities for navigating future challenges. You'll develop your early warning system, create intervention strategies, strengthen your support network, and plan for continued growth beyond these eight weeks.

Day 1–2: Early Warning System Development

Personal Pattern Analysis. Review your experience from the past seven weeks to identify your unique patterns:

- What are your most reliable early warning signs for anxiety, depression, and anger?
- Which situations, relationships, or stressors most consistently trigger old patterns?
- How much time typically passes between early warning signs and full activation?
- What patterns tend to emerge during stress, illness, or major life changes?

Somatic Early Warning Mapping. Create a detailed map of your physical early warning signs:

For Anxiety:

- First physical signs (breathing changes, muscle tension, heart rate).
- Progressive symptoms as activation increases.
- Point of no return where intervention becomes more difficult.
- Physical sensations that indicate successful intervention.

For Depression:

- Initial energy or postural changes.
- Early signs of withdrawal or isolation impulses.
- Physical indicators of hope vs. hopelessness.
- Bodily sensations that indicate lifting depression.

For Anger:

- First signs of heat, tension, or mobilization.
- Progressive activation patterns.
- Physical indicators of constructive vs. destructive anger.
- Somatic signs that anger is being channeled effectively.

Trigger Situation Assessment. Identify specific situations that activate your patterns:

- Interpersonal dynamics that trigger attachment wounds.
- Work or family stressors that overwhelm your capacity.
- Cultural or identity situations that activate trauma or stress.
- Environmental factors that affect your nervous system regulation.

Early Warning Practice. Develop a daily practice of checking in with your early warning systems:

- Morning assessment of your current state and potential triggers for the day.
- Midday check-in with your nervous system and emotional state.
- Evening review of early warning signs you noticed and how you responded.

Key Goal: Develop sophisticated awareness of your unique early warning signs and trigger patterns.

Day 3–4: Intervention Strategy Tool Kit

Current Intervention Assessment: Evaluate the effectiveness of strategies you've developed:

- Which somatic practices are most effective for different emotional states?
- What cognitive strategies help you maintain perspective during challenges?
- Which relational approaches help you stay connected during stress?
- What meaning-making practices help you find purpose in difficulties?

Intervention Strategy Development: Create specific intervention protocols for different scenarios:

Yellow Zone Interventions (Early Activation):

- Three to five-minute practices that can shift nervous system state before overwhelm.
- Cognitive strategies that work when you still have good prefrontal cortex function.
- Relational approaches for seeking support before crisis.
- Environmental modifications that support regulation.

Red Zone Interventions (High Activation):

- Crisis management techniques that work even during intense emotional states.
- Grounding practices that can anchor you during overwhelm.
- Safety planning for when emotions feel dangerous or overwhelming.
- Emergency support protocols for accessing help quickly

Recovery Zone Interventions (Post-Crisis):

- Practices for processing intense experiences without re-traumatization.

- Integration approaches that help you learn from difficult episodes.
- Self-compassion practices for handling post-crisis shame or judgment.
- Re-engagement strategies for gradually returning to normal activities

Situation-Specific Interventions. Develop specialized approaches for your most common triggers:

- Workplace stress management.
- Family conflict navigation.
- Financial or practical crisis management.
- Health or medical challenge support.
- Discrimination or identity-based stress response.

Intervention Practice: Role-play or mentally rehearse using your intervention strategies in different scenarios.

Key Goal: Develop a comprehensive tool kit of intervention strategies for different levels of activation and different triggering situations.

Day 5–6: Support Network Development and Strengthening

Current Support Network Assessment. Map your existing support system:

- **Emotional Support**: People you can be authentic with about your struggles and growth.
- **Practical Support**: People who can help with your concrete needs during challenges.
- **Professional Support**: Therapists, coaches, or medical providers who understand your approach.

- **Community Support**: Groups, organizations, or communities that share your values.
- **Co-Regulation Support**: People whose presence helps regulate your nervous system.

Support Network Gaps. Identify areas where your support system could be strengthened:

- What types of support do you need that you don't currently have?
- Which relationships provide support but lack reciprocity?
- What professional support would benefit your continued growth?
- How could you better utilize the support that's already available?

Support Network Building. Take concrete steps to strengthen your support system:

- Reach out to one person you'd like to develop a deeper relationship with.
- Research therapists, support groups, or professional resources in your area.
- Join one community or organization that aligns with your values.
- Practice asking for specific support from people in your existing network.

Reciprocal Support Development. Focus on creating mutual, sustainable support relationships:

- Practice offering support to others without depleting yourself.

- Learn to receive support gracefully without feeling indebted.
- Develop relationships where both people can be authentic about challenges.
- Create boundaries that protect everyone's capacity and energy.

Crisis Support Planning. Develop specific plans for accessing support during difficulties:

- Create a list of people to call during different types of crises.
- Establish protocols for when and how to reach out for professional help.
- Develop emergency self-care plans that include support activation.
- Practice asking for help before you're in crisis.

Key Goal: Develop a robust, reciprocal support network that can sustain you through ongoing challenges and growth.

Day 7: Continuous Growth Planning and Integration

Transformation Review. Reflect on your growth over the past eight weeks:

- How have your relationships with anxiety, depression, and anger shifted?
- What somatic awareness and regulation skills have become most natural?
- How has your capacity for authentic expression and healthy boundaries developed?
- What meaning and purpose have emerged from your integration work?

Ongoing Growth Areas. Identify areas where you want to continue developing:

- Which integration skills would benefit from deeper development?
- What new challenges or growth edges are emerging in your life?
- How can you continue to deepen your somatic awareness and emotional intelligence?
- What aspects of relational or meaning-making work call for continued attention?

Continuous Learning Plan. Create specific plans for ongoing development:

- **Books, courses, or trainings** that would support your continued growth.
- **Practice groups or communities** where you can continue developing skills.
- **Professional support** that would benefit your ongoing integration.
- **Mentorship opportunities** either as mentor or mentee.

Life Integration Planning. Plan for how to integrate your learning into major life areas:

- **Work/Career**: How will you bring embodied awareness to professional life?
- **Relationships**: How will you apply your learning to family and friendships?
- **Parenting**: How will you use embodied approaches with children (if applicable)?
- **Community**: How will you contribute your skills to broader community healing?

Challenge Preparation. Anticipate and prepare for future challenges:

- What predictable stressors or challenges can you prepare for?
- Which old patterns are most likely to resurface during stress?
- What additional support might you need for anticipated challenges?
- How can you maintain your practices during busy or difficult periods?

Legacy and Contribution Planning. Consider how your healing contributes to larger healing:

- How does your personal integration affect family patterns and relationships?
- What opportunities exist to share your learning with others on similar journeys?
- How can your embodied resilience contribute to positive social change?
- What gifts has your healing journey revealed that you can offer to the world?

Commitment and Intention Setting. Make specific commitments for your ongoing journey:

- Daily practices you'll maintain to support continued integration.
- Weekly or monthly practices for ongoing growth and development.
- Annual intentions for deepening your embodied emotional intelligence.
- Ways you'll contribute your healing to collective healing.

Weekly Success Metrics

By the end of Week 8, you should be able to:

- Recognize your early warning signs for emotional dysregulation before they become overwhelming.
- Access effective intervention strategies for different levels of activation and different triggering situations.
- Utilize a supportive network of relationships that enhance your resilience.
- Have a concrete plan for continuing your growth and integration beyond these eight weeks.
- Celebrate your transformation while maintaining realistic expectations for ongoing development.

Troubleshooting Common Challenges

"I'm worried I'll lose my progress without the structure of the program." The skills you've developed are now part of your nervous system and will remain available. Create your own ongoing structure through daily practices and regular check-ins.

"I still feel anxious/depressed/angry sometimes." This is normal and expected. The goal wasn't to eliminate these emotions but to develop a different relationship with them. Notice how your responses have changed even if the feelings still arise.

"I don't feel ready to handle major challenges." Resilience develops through practice, not through feeling ready. Start with smaller challenges and build capacity gradually. Remember that seeking support is part of resilience, not a sign of failure.

"I'm not sure how to maintain my support network." Relationships require ongoing attention and reciprocity.

Schedule regular check-ins with supportive people, offer support to others, and be patient as relationships deepen over time.

Guided Embodied Resilience Integration Session: Celebrating Your Journey and Preparing for What's Ahead

Allow approximately 30–35 minutes for this final integration session. This practice celebrates your transformation while preparing you for the ongoing journey of embodied emotional intelligence.

Find a position that feels both grounded and open—perhaps sitting with your spine straight, your feet connected to the earth, and your heart open to possibility. Since this is our final guided practice together, choose a space where you feel safe to reflect on your journey and set intentions for your continued growth.

Take a moment to acknowledge the profound courage it has taken to complete this 8-week journey of emotional transformation. In a culture that often encourages emotional avoidance or superficial quick fixes, you have chosen the path of deep integration, somatic awareness, and authentic self-development.

Begin with several natural breaths, feeling your body's familiar rhythm of expansion and release. Notice how your breathing has become an ally over these past weeks—not just an automatic function, but a doorway to presence, regulation, and choice.

Let's start by honoring the journey you've traveled. Eight weeks ago, you began this exploration with your own unique patterns of depression, anxiety, and anger. Take a moment to remember who you were at the beginning of this process. What was your relationship with these emotions? How did they feel in your body? What patterns of thinking, relating, and living did they create?

Without judgment, simply acknowledge that earlier version of yourself with compassion. That person was doing their best with the tools they had available. They had the wisdom to seek transformation and the courage to begin this journey.

Now, bring your awareness to who you are today. Notice how your relationship with difficult emotions has shifted. You may still feel anxiety, depression, or anger, but how has your response to these feelings changed? How has your capacity to stay present with challenging emotions expanded?

Feel in your body the somatic awareness you've developed—your ability to read the signals your nervous system sends, to recognize early warning signs before they become overwhelming, and to use your breath and body wisdom to guide your responses to life's challenges.

Appreciate the emotional intelligence you've cultivated—your growing capacity to hear the messages within difficult emotions, to use feelings as information rather than being overwhelmed by them, and to transform emotional energy into fuel for authentic action.

Acknowledge the relational skills you've developed—your increased ability to express your authentic needs, to set boundaries with compassion, to seek support when needed, and to offer support to others without losing yourself.

Recognize the meaning and purpose that has emerged through your healing journey—how your struggles have become sources of wisdom, how your healing contributes to something larger than yourself, and how your transformation affects not just you but everyone whose life you touch.

Now let's connect with the embodied resilience you've built. Bring to mind a recent challenge you navigated—it doesn't have to be dramatic, just something that would have previously overwhelmed you or activated old patterns.

Notice how you responded differently than you might have eight weeks ago. Perhaps you caught early warning signs before they became overwhelming. Maybe you used intervention strategies to maintain your regulation. You might have reached out for support or channeled difficult emotions into constructive action.

Feel in your body the difference between your old patterns and your new capacities. This is embodied resilience—not the absence of challenges, but the presence of skills, awareness, and resources that allow you to navigate difficulties while maintaining connection to your authentic self.

Let's acknowledge the support network you've been building. Bring to mind the people who have supported your journey—friends, family members, professionals, or community members who have encouraged your growth or provided co-regulation during difficult times.

Feel your gratitude for these relationships, and also feel your own capacity to offer support to others. Notice how your healing has increased your ability to be present with others' difficulties without being overwhelmed, to offer wisdom gained through your own struggles, and to contribute to collective healing through your individual transformation.

Now let's look toward the future with realistic hope. Your journey of embodied emotional intelligence is not ending—it's transitioning from a structured 8-week program to a lifelong practice of ongoing growth and deepening integration.

Imagine yourself six months from now, continuing to apply and deepen these skills. See yourself navigating future challenges with even greater skill and wisdom. Visualize the relationships you'll build, the contributions you'll make, and the ways your continued healing will ripple out to benefit others.

Picture yourself a year from now, with even more sophisticated capacities for emotional intelligence, somatic awareness, and authentic living. See yourself perhaps supporting others on similar journeys, contributing your unique gifts to community healing, and living more fully aligned with your deepest values and purpose.

This is not fantasy—this is the natural trajectory of embodied growth when supported by consistent practice and genuine commitment to transformation.

Set an intention for your ongoing journey. What aspects of embodied emotional intelligence do you want to continue developing? How do you want to contribute your healing to the larger healing of the world? What support do you need to maintain your growth and continue expanding your capacities?

Now, let's create what I call your "resilience anchor"—a felt sense memory you can return to whenever you need to remember your strength and capacity. Bring to mind the moment in these past eight weeks when you felt most integrated, most capable, and most like your authentic self.

This might have been a moment when you successfully navigated a trigger without being overwhelmed, when you expressed an authentic need with skill and courage, when you felt your emotions as allies rather than enemies, or when you experienced deep connection to meaning and purpose.

Don't just remember this moment—feel it in your body. Notice your posture, your breathing, and the quality of energy and presence you embodied. Feel the confidence, the aliveness, and the sense of being fully yourself.

This embodied memory is always available to you. During future challenges, you can return to this felt sense to remember who you truly are beneath any temporary emotional storms. This is your resilience anchor—proof that transformation is not only possible but already accomplished within you.

Let's practice accessing this anchor. Imagine a future challenge—nothing overwhelming, just something that might typically trigger old patterns. Now, connect with your resilience anchor while holding this imagined challenge in awareness.

Notice how different the challenge feels when you approach it from your integrated, embodied self rather than from old patterns of reactivity. Feel how your nervous system remains more regulated, how your thinking stays clearer, and how your access to resources and support remains available.

This is embodied resilience in action—not the absence of challenges, but the presence of capacity to meet whatever arises while remaining connected to your authentic self.

As we prepare to complete this final guided session, take a moment to appreciate the mystery and wonder of transformation. Eight weeks ago, the capacities you now embody might have seemed impossible. Yet here you are, having literally rewired your nervous system, developed new emotional intelligence, and built sustainable practices for ongoing growth.

You have not just learned techniques—you have become someone new. Someone who can feel difficult emotions without being overwhelmed by them. Someone who can use body wisdom to guide decision-making. Someone who can maintain authentic relationships while honoring personal boundaries. Someone who can find meaning and purpose even within life's inevitable difficulties.

This transformation is not just personal—it's part of the larger healing of our world. Every time you choose presence over reactivity, authenticity over people-pleasing, and connection over isolation, you contribute to collective healing. Your individual integration supports the possibility of collective integration.

Set a final intention for carrying this work forward. Perhaps it's to maintain your daily practices with consistency and self-compassion. Maybe it's to continue seeking community and support for your ongoing growth. It might be to share your learning with others who are struggling with similar challenges.

Whatever your intention, feel it not just as a mental commitment but as a full-body dedication to continued growth, service, and authentic living.

Remember that this is not the end of your journey but a graduation to the next level of embodied emotional intelligence. You now have foundational skills that will continue to deepen and evolve throughout your life. You have tools that will serve you through whatever challenges and opportunities await.

Most importantly, you have proven to yourself that transformation is possible, that healing is real, that you have the capacity to navigate life's difficulties while remaining connected to what matters most.

As you prepare to leave this guided session and continue your independent journey, carry with you the felt sense of your own resilience, the appreciation for how far you've come, and the excitement for continued growth and contribution.

Take a few more conscious breaths, gently move your body, and slowly return your attention to the space around you. You are ready for whatever comes next, equipped not just with techniques but with embodied wisdom, authentic relationships, and an unshakable connection to your own capacity for growth and healing.

The journey continues, and you are prepared to meet it with grace, skill, and the profound knowing that you are capable of far more than you ever imagined possible.

Welcome to the rest of your integrated, embodied, resilient life.

Conclusion: The Ongoing Journey of Embodied Emotional Intelligence

As you complete this 8-week protocol, you are not finishing your emotional healing journey—you are graduating to a new level of embodied wisdom and resilience. The skills you have developed are not temporary techniques but permanent capacities that will continue to evolve and deepen throughout your life.

You began this journey with depression, anxiety, and anger as seemingly separate problems to be solved. You are completing it with the understanding that these emotions are interconnected expressions of mind-body disconnection that become allies when approached with somatic awareness, emotional intelligence, relational wisdom, and connection to meaning.

The transformation you have experienced is both deeply personal and inherently collective. Your individual healing contributes to the healing of family patterns, community dynamics, and the larger cultural shift toward more embodied, integrated ways of being human.

Your Ongoing Commitment

Your commitment now is not to perfection but to continuation—showing up for yourself with consistency and compassion, continuing to learn and grow, seeking support when needed, and offering your gifts to others when appropriate.

The practices you have learned will evolve as you evolve. Your morning integration may become more sophisticated. Your intervention strategies may become more nuanced. Your support network may expand and deepen. Your contribution to collective healing may grow in ways you cannot yet imagine.

The Ripple Effects of Your Transformation

Remember that your healing has effects far beyond your individual experience. Children who grow up with emotionally integrated adults learn different patterns. Relationships with partners, friends, and colleagues shift when one person develops greater emotional intelligence. Communities benefit when members can navigate conflict with skill and maintain connection across differences.

Your journey through these eight weeks has created ripples that will continue expanding throughout your lifetime and beyond. You are part of a growing movement of people choosing embodied emotional intelligence over reactive patterns, authentic connection over defensive isolation, and meaningful contribution over self-centered consumption.

The Path Forward

As you continue this journey, remember:

- **Progress, not perfection**: Growth continues throughout your lifetime. There will be setbacks, challenges, and times when old patterns resurface. This is normal and expected.
- **Integration over achievement**: The goal is not to reach a final state of emotional mastery but to continue deepening your capacity for working skillfully with whatever arises.
- **Community over isolation**: Healing happens in relationships. Continue building and maintaining connections that support your growth and allow you to support others' journeys.
- **Service over self-focus**: Your healing is not just for you. Look for ways to contribute your growing wisdom to the healing of others and the world.
- **Patience over urgency**: True transformation happens gradually, through consistent practice over time. Trust the process and be gentle with yourself.

You have completed something remarkable. You have chosen growth over stagnation, integration over fragmentation, and embodied wisdom over disembodied reactivity. You have developed capacities that will serve you for the rest of your life and contribute to healing that extends far beyond your individual experience.

The journey continues, and you are beautifully equipped to meet whatever comes next with skill, wisdom, and the profound knowing that you have everything you need within you to navigate life's challenges while remaining connected to what matters most.

Congratulations on your transformation. Welcome to the ongoing adventure of embodied emotional intelligence!

Chapter 12

Real Stories of Transformation

Embodied emotional intelligence creates profound, lasting change when practiced consistently over time.

The journey through somatic awareness, nervous system regulation, emotional integration, mind-body connection, relational healing, meaning-making, sustainable daily practices, and embodied resilience isn't just theoretical knowledge—it's a practical blueprint that transforms lives when applied holistically. While individual techniques from earlier chapters can provide relief, the real magic happens when someone embraces the entire integrated approach, allowing each element to support and amplify the others.

When I began developing this protocol eight years ago, I made the same promises to early participants that I've made to you throughout this book: that you can transform your relationship with depression, anxiety, and anger from adversarial to collaborative; that you can develop embodied wisdom that guides you through life's challenges; that you can create authentic relationships based on mutual support rather than codependency or isolation; and that you can discover meaning and purpose that sustain you through difficulties while contributing to something larger than yourself.

Jake's Complete Transformation: From Numbing to Integration

Jake's story demonstrates the profound transformation possible when someone commits to the entire integrated approach rather than seeking quick fixes. At 24, Jake was caught in what seemed like an inescapable cycle—crushing depression that made getting out of bed feel impossible, anxiety that would spike unpredictably, leaving him shaking and unable to concentrate, and explosive anger that damaged his relationships and left him feeling ashamed and more isolated than ever.

Jake's solution had been simple: numb it all. A few beers after work became a six-pack. Weekend drinking became weeknight drinking. When beer wasn't enough, he'd add pills—whatever he could find to quiet the emotional chaos in his chest. "I just want to feel normal," he'd tell himself, not understanding that he was at war with his own emotional intelligence.

Jake's transformation began when he stopped trying to silence his emotional messengers and started learning to understand their language. Through the eight-week protocol, he discovered that his depression wasn't random sadness—it was his system's way of saying he needed rest, connection, and time to grieve losses he'd never acknowledged, including his father's death two years earlier. His anxiety wasn't weakness—it was his body's attempt to alert him to boundary violations and situations where his safety or values were being compromised. His anger wasn't just destructive rage—it was his authentic self fighting to be seen, heard, and respected.

The breakthrough came during Week 3 when Jake learned to sit with emotions instead of immediately reaching for substances. The first time he felt depression arise, instead of drinking it away, he spent five minutes simply experiencing it in his body. What he discovered amazed him: underneath the familiar weight was grief for his father, exhaustion from trying to be someone he wasn't, and a deep longing for life to have meaning.

Jake's somatic awareness development helped him recognize that his emotions had specific physical signatures. Depression felt like heaviness in his chest and a collapse in his posture. Anxiety manifested as tightness that began around his heart and spread through his arms as restless energy. Anger appeared as jaw clenching and heat rising from his belly. These became early warning signals rather than overwhelming storms.

By Week 4, Jake had developed what he called his "integration practices"—ways of working with thoughts and physical sensations as one unified system. When anxiety began to spike at work, he could breathe into his chest while acknowledging that his system was trying to prepare him for challenges. When depression threatened, he could honor the need for rest while staying connected to supportive relationships.

The relational healing work in Week 5 transformed Jake's capacity for authentic connection. Instead of emotional withdrawal or explosive outbursts, he learned to express his needs directly. His relationship with his girlfriend deepened as he shared his grief about his father rather than numbing it with alcohol. His friendships became more genuine as he stopped pretending everything was fine and started asking for support when needed.

Jake's discovery of meaning during Week 6 provided the foundation for sustainable change. He realized that his struggles with addiction and mental health had given him unique understanding that could help others. He began volunteering with a peer support program for young adults dealing with substance use, finding that helping others gave his own recovery a profound purpose.

The daily practices Jake developed during Week 7 were designed to work with his real life as a working tradesman. His morning routine consisted of three conscious breaths and asking his body what it needed that day. His midday resets involved brief check-ins during lunch breaks. His evening practice included processing the day's emotions through journaling and appreciating his growth.

Jake's embodied resilience was tested six months later when work stress intensified and relationship conflicts arose. The old Jake would have reached for alcohol immediately. Instead, he was able to recognize his early warning signs, use his intervention techniques, and reach out for support before patterns became overwhelming. His drinking decreased naturally as he developed these skills—not through willpower but because he no longer needed to numb emotions that had become his allies.

Today, eighteen months later, Jake describes his transformation as "learning to live in my body instead of fighting it." He still experiences depression, anxiety, and anger, but these emotions move through him rather than getting stuck. His relationship with his girlfriend has deepened into engagement. His work performance has improved as he's learned to channel emotional energy constructively. Most remarkably, Jake has become a mentor in the peer support program, helping other young adults discover that their emotions can be allies rather than enemies.

Maria's Journey: Healing Intergenerational Trauma

Maria's story illustrates how the protocol can address not just individual emotional patterns but generational trauma passed down through families. At 35, Maria carried the weight of childhood experiences with an alcoholic father and depressed mother, patterns that had shaped her into a hypervigilant, people-pleasing adult who lived in constant fear of abandonment while simultaneously pushing people away.

Maria's nervous system had learned early that survival meant predicting danger, staying small, and never expecting safety. By age eight, she was scanning her parents' faces for signs of the next explosion or shutdown. By twelve, she'd internalized the message that her needs were burdens and that love had to be earned through perfect behavior.

As an adult, Maria understood intellectually that these childhood messages were no longer accurate. As a social worker, she could explain trauma responses to clients with expertise and compassion. But when triggered, her body would respond as if she were still that frightened child, and her mind would flood with the same survival thoughts that had once kept her safe but now kept her trapped.

Maria's transformation began during Week 1 when she learned to recognize how childhood trauma lived in her present-day body. The thought "I'm not safe" always appeared with tension in her upper back and shoulders hunching forward. The thought "I'm too much for people" came with a collapse in her chest and a pulling inward of her arms. More importantly, she noticed that these physical patterns often preceded the thoughts—her body was responding to environmental cues that reminded her unconsciously of childhood experiences.

The somatic cognitive integration work of Week 4 became transformative for Maria. Instead of trying to think her way out of trauma responses, she learned what she called "somatic cognitive restructuring." When she noticed her body beginning to contract with the familiar "I'm not safe" pattern, she would:

1. Acknowledge the body pattern: "I notice my shoulders hunching and my chest tightening."

2. Recognize the thought pattern: "The story 'I'm not safe' is arising."

3. Provide somatic resources: Consciously soften her shoulders, breathe into her chest, and feel her feet on the ground.

4. Offer updated information: "I notice this pattern from childhood. Right now, in this moment, I can create safety by breathing and grounding."

The integration worked both ways. As Maria's body learned to relax and open, her thoughts naturally became more flexible and optimistic. As she developed cognitive awareness of her trauma patterns, she could use that awareness to guide somatic interventions before the patterns became overwhelming.

Maria's relational healing involved learning to distinguish between her adult self and her childhood trauma responses. In relationships, she learned to recognize when her hypervigilance was responding to past rather than present dynamics. She developed the capacity to stay present during conflict without reverting to childhood survival strategies of people-pleasing or emotional withdrawal.

The meaning-making work helped Maria understand that her childhood experiences, while painful, had given her unique wisdom about resilience and healing that could benefit others in her social work practice. Instead of seeing her trauma history as a liability, she began to recognize it as a source of professional strength and authentic connection with clients.

Maria's daily practices incorporated trauma-informed approaches that honored her nervous system's need for safety and gradual healing. Her morning routine included grounding exercises that helped her feel safe in her body. Her midday practices involved boundary-checking to ensure she wasn't taking on clients' trauma. Her evening routine included specific practices for processing any trauma activation from her workday.

The embodied resilience Maria developed was tested during a particularly triggering period when workplace conflicts activated her childhood patterns around criticism and rejection. Instead of reverting to hypervigilance and people-pleasing, Maria was able to recognize her trauma responses, provide appropriate self-care, and address the workplace issues from her adult capacity rather than her traumatized child self.

Two years later, Maria has become a leader in trauma-informed social work practice. Her personal healing journey has enhanced her professional effectiveness, allowing her to work with traumatized clients from a place of integrated wisdom rather than unhealed wounds. Her romantic relationship has deepened as she's learned to recognize and communicate her needs without the intensity of childhood trauma. Most significantly, Maria reports feeling "at home in my body" for the first time in her adult life.

Marcus's Integrated Approach: From Individual Pain to Community Healing

Marcus's story demonstrates how personal healing and collective contribution can become inseparable when approached through integrated practices. At 42, Marcus had achieved external success as an architect but felt completely empty inside. His depression made everything feel pointless despite professional recognition. His anxiety about performance and reputation felt increasingly meaningless. His anger at clients and colleagues consumed energy that might otherwise flow toward meaningful work.

The turning point came during a panic attack in his office when Marcus looked around at his awards, expensive furniture, and portfolio of impressive buildings and realized he felt no connection to any of it. These achievements belonged to someone he had created to be successful, but they had nothing to do with who he actually was or what truly mattered to him.

Marcus's somatic awareness development helped him recognize that his emotional suffering wasn't random mental illness—it was his soul's rebellion against a life that had become disconnected from meaning. His depression wasn't just sadness; it was grief for the dreams he'd abandoned. His anxiety wasn't just stress; it was his system's alarm about living inauthentically. His anger wasn't just irritation; it was his authentic self fighting for recognition and expression.

The emotional integration work of Week 3 helped Marcus understand his emotions as messengers rather than problems. His depression was calling him to slow down and reconsider his priorities. His anxiety was questioning whether he was living authentically. His anger was providing energy to advocate for what he believed in—sustainable design practices and community-centered architecture.

Marcus's journey through meaning and purpose in Week 6 became the foundation for everything else. Instead of designing buildings purely for profit or prestige, Marcus began focusing on how his architectural work could serve human flourishing. He started incorporating more natural light, community spaces, and sustainable materials. He volunteered his skills for nonprofit organizations, designing community gardens and affordable housing projects.

The changes in Marcus's emotional state were dramatic. The depression that had felt so heavy began to lift as he reconnected with work that aligned with his values. His anxiety about performance decreased as he focused on internal alignment rather than external validation. His anger transformed from destructive frustration into constructive energy for advocating for sustainable and community-centered design.

Marcus's daily practices became integrated with his professional life rather than separate from it. His morning routine involved setting intentions for how his work could serve human well-being. His midday practices included brief connections to his values and purpose. His evening routine involved appreciating the ways his work had contributed to something larger than himself.

The embodied resilience Marcus developed allowed him to maintain his integrated approach even during professional challenges. When clients criticized his more values-based designs, Marcus could stay centered because he knew his work was serving something larger than just profit or recognition. When industry pressures mounted, he could use his emotional responses as information about whether opportunities aligned with his authentic values.

Marcus has since become a leader in sustainable architecture and community design. He mentors young architects interested in socially conscious work and has presented at conferences about architecture as a form of social healing. His personal transformation has become inseparable from his professional contribution, demonstrating how individual integration can serve collective healing.

His marriage has strengthened as he's learned to bring the same authenticity to his personal relationships that he brought to his work. His children are growing up with a father who models the integration of personal values with professional contribution, showing them that work can be a form of service rather than just obligation.

The Common Elements of Transformation

These three stories, while unique in their details, share several common elements that illuminate how integrated transformation occurs:

Holistic Rather Than Fragmented Approach: Each person worked with depression, anxiety, and anger as interconnected expressions of mind-body disconnection rather than separate problems requiring separate solutions. Jake learned that numbing one emotion meant numbing them all. Maria discovered that her trauma responses affected her entire nervous system. Marcus realized that his professional emptiness was connected to emotional and spiritual disconnection.

Body Wisdom as Foundation: All three developed sophisticated somatic awareness that became their foundation for emotional regulation, decision-making, and authentic living. Their bodies became allies and sources of information rather than enemies to overcome.

Emotions as Messengers: Each person learned to work with difficult emotions as sources of information and energy rather than obstacles to eliminate. Their depression, anxiety, and anger became guides for authentic living rather than signs of personal failure.

Integration Over Management: Instead of managing symptoms, each person transformed their fundamental relationship with emotional experience. They developed the capacity to feel fully while maintaining choice in how they responded.

Trauma-Informed Healing: For those with trauma histories like Maria, the approach honored protective responses while creating new options, working with the nervous system's wisdom rather than overriding it.

Meaning-Making: Each person's healing became connected to larger purposes—Jake's peer support work, Maria's trauma-informed practice, and Marcus's community-centered architecture. Personal healing and collective contribution became inseparable.

Sustainable Daily Practices: All three developed practices that could survive real-life demands rather than requiring ideal circumstances. Their healing became integrated into daily life rather than dependent on special conditions.

Embodied Resilience: Each person developed the capacity to navigate challenges while maintaining a connection to their authentic self, using difficulties as opportunities for growth rather than evidence of failure.

Getting Started: Your Path to Integration

If you're inspired by these stories and ready to begin your own journey of embodied emotional intelligence, here are the most effective starting points based on these successful transformations:

Start with Somatic Awareness: Like Jake, develop the foundation skill of recognizing how emotions show up in your unique body. Practice the body scan and sensation tracking exercises from Week 1. This single skill will give you more choice in how you respond to emotional experiences.

Understand Your Emotions as Messengers: Follow Maria's example of learning to decode what your emotions are trying to communicate rather than fighting or numbing them. Use the emotional integration practices from Week 3 to work with emotions as allies.

Connect to Authentic Meaning: Like Marcus, explore how your current life aligns with your deepest values and authentic calling. Use the meaning and purpose practices from Week 6 to discover how your healing can serve something larger than individual concerns.

Then, as these foundational skills become natural, gradually add:

Nervous System Regulation: Learn techniques for shifting from states of overwhelm or shutdown back to presence and choice, using the practices from Week 2.

Somatic Cognitive Integration: Develop skills for working with thoughts and physical sensations as one unified system, as Maria learned in Week 4.

Relational Healing: Build capacity for authentic expression and healthy boundaries using the relational skills from Week 5.

Sustainable Daily Practices: Create simple, consistent practices that can survive real-life demands, following the guidance from Week 7.

Embodied Resilience: Develop the capacity to thrive through challenges while maintaining connection to your authentic self, using the approaches from Week 8.

The most important insight from all three stories is this: transformation happens through integration, not perfection. Jake didn't eliminate his emotions—he learned to work with them. Maria didn't erase her trauma history—she integrated it into wisdom. Marcus didn't achieve perfect work-life balance—he found ways to align his entire life with his authentic values.

Your path to embodied emotional intelligence is not about becoming someone different—it's about becoming more fully yourself. The same capacity for integration that transformed Jake's addiction, Maria's trauma, and Marcus's emptiness is available to you, beginning with your willingness to approach your emotions as allies rather than enemies.

The stories you've read are not about exceptional people with special gifts. They are about ordinary humans who chose to engage consistently with the practices of integration and discovered an extraordinary capacity for resilience, wisdom, and authentic living. The same transformation awaits you, beginning with your next conscious breath, your next moment of body awareness, and your next choice to listen to your emotions' messages with curiosity rather than judgment.

Your journey of embodied emotional intelligence starts now, and it has the potential to transform not only your individual experience but also to contribute to the healing of your family, community, and world. The practices are simple, the results are profound, and the capacity is yours to develop.

Chapter 13

Your Journey Begins Now—Stepping Into Embodied Emotional Intelligence

When you first picked up this book, you wondered if it was really possible to transform your relationship with depression, anxiety, and anger. Perhaps you felt exhausted by the endless cycle of these emotions controlling your life, skeptical that another approach could make a difference, or desperate enough to try anything that might offer genuine relief. You may have been tired of treating these feelings as separate enemies to battle, frustrated with solutions that provided only temporary relief, or questioning whether lasting emotional healing was even possible for someone like you. You picked up this book because something deep inside you knew that the way you'd been struggling with emotions wasn't working, and you were ready—perhaps cautiously, perhaps desperately—to consider a radically different approach.

Through taking action on the principles and practices outlined in the previous chapters, you will manifest the promises I made to you at the beginning of this journey. You will transform your relationship with depression, anxiety, and anger from adversarial to collaborative, discovering that these emotions carry valuable information about your needs, boundaries, and authentic self. You will develop embodied wisdom that allows you to feel difficult emotions without being overwhelmed by them, using your body's intelligence to guide decisions and responses. You will create authentic relationships based on mutual support rather than codependency or people-pleasing, learning to express your needs clearly while maintaining healthy boundaries. You will discover meaning and purpose that sustain you through life's inevitable difficulties while contributing to healing that extends far beyond your individual experience. Most profoundly, you will develop what I call "embodied emotional intelligence"—the capacity to live as an integrated being where mind and body work together harmoniously, where emotions become allies rather than enemies, and where challenges become opportunities for growth rather than evidence of failure.

Let me share with you the story of Elena, whose transformation embodies every promise this book has made. When Elena first approached me, she was drowning in what felt like a perfect storm of life challenges. As a single mother and nurse, she was already stretched thin when multiple crises converged: her daughter's chronic illness diagnosis, her mother's injury requiring care, massive layoffs at her hospital, car repairs she couldn't afford, and her ex-husband's sudden custody demands. Elena's immediate thought was that all her previous healing work had been useless—she was right back where she started with familiar anxiety symptoms, explosive anger, and moments of crushing depression.

But something remarkable happened. Instead of being completely derailed as she would have been in the past, Elena found herself responding from a deeper place of strength she didn't know she possessed. Her seven weeks of integration practice had created what she called "emotional muscle memory." Even when her conscious mind was overwhelmed, her body remembered how to find its center. She could feel anxiety in her chest and breathe with it instead of being consumed by it. She could channel anger into advocacy for her daughter rather than explosive conflicts. Even depression became a teacher, forcing her to slow down and prioritize what truly mattered.

Elena discovered that embodied resilience isn't about never having problems—it's about having a relationship with problems that doesn't destroy you. Her anxiety became an alert system for what needed attention. Her anger provided energy to fight for what mattered. Her depression showed her what needed to be released and what deserved protection. Today, Elena describes her life as fundamentally transformed not because she eliminated difficult emotions, but because she learned to work with them as allies in creating an authentic, meaningful life.

The big picture action steps that will create this transformation in your own life follow a clear, progressive path. Begin with developing somatic awareness—the foundational skill of recognizing how emotions show up in your unique body, creating early warning systems that give you choice in how you respond. Build nervous system regulation capacity through practices that help you shift from states of overwhelm or shutdown back to presence and choice. Develop emotional integration skills that allow you to work with depression, anxiety, and anger as messengers rather than problems to eliminate. Create somatic cognitive integration by learning to work with thoughts and physical sensations as one unified system rather than separate, competing forces. Heal relational patterns by developing capacity for authentic expression, healthy boundaries, and mutual support. Connect with meaning and purpose that align your daily life with your deepest values and contribution to something larger than individual concerns. Establish sustainable daily practices that can survive real-life demands rather than requiring perfect circumstances. Finally, build embodied resilience—the capacity to navigate life's inevitable challenges while maintaining connection to your authentic, integrated self.

You can put this into action starting right now, this very moment. Choose one practice from Week 1 and commit to it for the next seven days—perhaps three conscious breaths upon waking, a brief body scan during lunch, or thirty seconds of gratitude before sleep. Set a daily reminder and show up consistently, not perfectly. As this practice becomes natural, add one element from Week 2, then Week 3, building gradually rather than trying to transform everything at once. Remember that sustainable change happens through small, consistent actions rather than dramatic overhauls. Trust that each moment of somatic awareness, each breath taken consciously, and each emotion met with curiosity rather than resistance is rewiring your nervous system and building capacity for embodied emotional intelligence. Most importantly, be patient and compassionate with yourself—this is not about perfection but about consistent engagement with practices that honor your whole self.

You have within you everything necessary to create the same transformation that Jake, Maria, Marcus, Elena, and countless others have experienced. Your depression carries wisdom about what needs to change in your life. Your anxiety holds information about what deserves your attention and protection. Your anger contains energy for defending your values and authentic self. Your body possesses remarkable intelligence for healing and regulation when you learn to listen to its signals. Your relationships have the potential to become sources of mutual support and authentic connection. Your life has meaning and purpose waiting to be discovered and expressed. You are not broken and do not need to be fixed—you are a complete, integrated being whose capacity for embodied emotional intelligence is your birthright. The same transformation that has changed thousands of lives is available to you, beginning with your next conscious breath, your next moment of self-compassion, and your next choice to work with your emotions as allies rather than enemies. Trust in your capacity for growth, believe in your worthiness of healing, and step boldly into the embodied, integrated life that awaits you.

Your journey of embodied emotional intelligence begins now, not when you feel ready, not when circumstances are perfect, but in this moment with whatever capacity you currently possess. The practices are simple, the results are profound, and the time is now. Your transformed life is calling—answer with courage, commitment, and the unshakable knowing that you are capable of far more healing, growth, and authentic living than you have yet imagined.

www.ingramcontent.com/pod-product-compliance
Lightning Source LLC
LaVergne TN
LVHW051824080426
835512LV00018B/2714